A Secured Framework for Enhanced and Efficient Communication in IoT Ecosystem

Saranya V S

A Secured Framework for Enhanced and Efficient Communication in IoT Ecosystem

First Edition February 2024

Written by Saranya V S

TABLE OF CONTENTS

LIST OF TABLES

LIST OF FIGURES

ABBREVIATIONS

AIFLS	AI based Fuzzy Logic Systems
CAGR	Compound Annual Growth Rate
CAV	Connected Autonomous Vehicles
DBN	Deep Belief Network
DDoS	Distributed Denial of Service
DoS	Denial of Service
DTL	Deep Transfer Learning
FLS	Fuzzy Logic Systems
FPT	Fuzzy Pattern Tree
IG	Information Gain
IoBT	Internet of Battlefield Things
IoMT	Internet of Medical Things
IoT	Internet of Things
PDoS	Permanent Denial of Service
QoS	Quality of Service

CHAPTER 1

INTRODUCTION

1.1 INTRODUCTION

IoT security technologies ensure the protection of devices and networks associated with Internet of Things (IoT) ecosystem. IoT affords internet connectivity amid various inter related devices. It presents a unique identification and automates data transfer within the network. There are possibilities for severe vulnerabilities for the devices which are allowed with internet connection. Back to back COVID -19 pandemic periods are challenging for various industries related to healthcare, retail, automotive and manufacturing.

However, IoT technology played a very important role in meeting the needs of business and customers. All the industries are evolved as smart because of the arrival of IoT. This integrated Artificial Intelligence technology and big data applied to tackle mass flooding of data in this 21st century. Various IoT devices and data centers are connected together to form IoT as an intelligent network. IoT devices are considered as connected devices which provide data analysis by making use of sensors.

Number of sensors is massive and they rely on power consumption and connectivity. There are possibilities for security and privacy breaches in IoT ecosystem as more amount of confidential and sensitive information is shared. Most of the IoT devices are independent and works with less human intervention. Few IoT devices are built with exclusive authentication based identification. Primary feature of IoT device is minimal energy consumption which affords data collection and sharing in remote areas.

IoT utilization is increased in AI, cloud computing, big data and smart systems like smart cities, smart offices and smart homes. A typical IoT system is defined with three primary steps which are data collection, data transfer and data analysis. First step is referred as physical layer where sensors and microcontrollers are used for collecting and diffusing data. IoT network components like hub or gateway are utilized for data transfer in second step. In third step, data analysis is implemented by consisting user interface and cloud like back end system. Violation occurrences in any of these three steps will reveal sensitive information of connected IoT devices. Several vulnerable exploitations are implied towards IoT devices because of its poor encryption and authentication system.

After COVID - 19 crisis and its severe impacts, growth of IoT market size is predicted as USD 650.5 billion in 2026 which was with the worth of USD 300.3 billion during 2021 (Hassan & Wan Haslina 2019). Compound Annual Growth Rate (CAGR) is expected as 16.7% for the same prediction period. COVID -19 analysis of IoT market is performed by considering various components (such as software solution, hardware and services), size of organization, focus area (like manufacturing, energy and utilities and retail in smart manner) and region. IoT market is comprised with the primary factors such as minimal cost access, least power consumption for sensors, accessibility with high speed connection, increased cloud adoptability and high utilization of data processing and analytics. Furthermore, increased universal smart city establishments, enormous growth of connected devices and promising 5G technologies require IoT implementation and business worldwide.

COVID - 19 pandemic crashed IoT market significantly. IoT sensors supply is impaired all over the world. In various projects, IoT and sensors deployment is stopped because of minimal personnel and hardware supply is also delayed. Stable development is observed for IoT platforms by concentrating infrastructure scaling by enterprises. Remote monitoring is utilized to provide software related solutions.

Software solutions require enlarged IoT operations deployment. Work From Home (WFH) system implementation is applied as the result of pandemic which makes demands in automation as well as remote management and it increased the priority of IoT systems to resolves the issues related to effective operation and minimal manpower. Various manufacturing plants obtained reduced production due to the pandemic's broken supply chain. IT related services are at the peak of the list of IoT market share holders and after that banking and financial services are following. Further, its market shares are expanded for the healthcare and government based applications with more percentage.

Considering the world's geographical regions, North America holds maximum contribution of universal IoT market where, US and Canada provide more investments for R&D establishments. Increased smart connected devices adoption and advanced technologies are playing key roles in IoT market. Asia Pacific region including Australia, Singapore, China, India and Japan affords profitable IT market by adopting advanced technologies with maximized growth rate. In January 2019, India invested INR 2 trillion for developing new 5000 smart city projects. As growth of IoT is enormous, it affords data sharing and communication for various applications by connecting billions of devices. In addition, such massive development leads to several securities and privacy based problems in IoT ecosystem and those issues should be considered and resolved primarily for effective and efficient IoT ecosystem.

According to the current report, global market value of IoT security is anticipated as $40.3 billion along with 22.1% CAGR by 2026 and it was recorded as $14.9 billion in the year 2021(Sfar *et al.,* 2018). Google, AWS, Microsoft, IBM, Ericsson, Cisco, and Thales are the key players of IoT security market with maximum shares. Most of the threats and exploitations are correlated with network security of IoT and its market value is also high.

Network security solutions are required for resolving increased cyber threats for all the enterprises. Complex architecture of IoT network is in danger forever. Due to the dynamicity of the network, attackers attempt vulnerable exploitations. Enormous amount of exploitations discovered in various fields like applications, devices, users and localities.

Various network security based tools and applications are available for dealing IoT vulnerabilities and threats. Large scaled organizations hold maximum market size and they are remodeling security architectures and policies for integrating big data in order to provide protection without attacks. Each and every large scaled enterprises combat against anonymous malware attacks in order to protect all the fields of ecosystem like IoT network, data center, user endpoint, devices and apps. Increased amount of advanced cyber-attacks enlarged the demands of IoT security solutions primarily for large scaled enterprises.

1.2 OBJECTIVE

The key objective of this research is to develop an efficient and robust security framework for IoT malware detection and security.

This dissertation holds three unique methods/schemes which are efficient and the major concerns addressed by the proposed framework are given below.

- To develop an autonomous malware detection and attack detection framework for IoT architecture

- An intelligent IoT attack detection framework using effective Edge AI based computing

- An automated security model for data driven IoT ecosystem

- Secured IoT malware detection framework using AI based Fuzzy Logic Systems

- A novel AI based framework is proposed which is of first kind to deploy in real time

1.3 ORGANIZATION AND SCOPE OF THEBOOK

The main scope of the book is to develop a reliable and optimal deep learning and AI framework for IoT malware and attack detection. The objective of this research is to build efficient algorithms for IoT malware and attack detection. The objective is achieved by building an effective and efficient detection framework. This dissertation proposes three novel schemes. The entire dissertation is sub-divided into 5 chapters.

Chapter 1 discusses the basics of IoT architecture and its related security techniques. Literature survey is discussed clearly in chapter 2. Here, various state of the art techniques involved in IoT security are also discussed.

In chapter 3, the proposed schemes are discussed. The observation is made on the three schemes. The first scheme employs an intelligent IoT attack detection framework. The key idea of the proposed scheme is to adopt edge computing to increase the speed of data processing in order to integrate the security essentials amid software applications and their associated networks. As this proposed framework is enabled with AI, discovering malicious threats become effective.

The second scheme takes advantage over the existing and conventional methodologies and leverages hybrid schemes by automated security model for data driven IoT ecosystem. The key idea is to ensure maximum security in data driven IoT systems which is a highly challengeable task. This chapter proposes an automated security model is proposed by adopting enhanced data analysis technique to recognize anomalies of the IoT system. This proposed security model is designed by integrating deep learning models and AI for identifying anomalies and abnormal behaviors in IoT ecosystem. As it is an AI enabled automated security model, manual intervention errors are avoided. Furthermore, optimal neural network model, auto encoder is used for classification.

Malware attacks on IoT devices are getting increased day by day. In recent times there is a new line of research which encountered by monitoring and analyzing the malware and its behavior very closely. IoT malwares are also evolved with the employment of advanced obfuscation and evading techniques. It is a very challengeable job for the security analysts as well as security providers. In this work, an enhanced IoT malware detection framework is proposed making use of AI based Fuzzy Logic Systems (AIFLS) by considering the shortcomings of existing recent detection methods. Fuzzy rules are generated automatically without any human intervention. Further, Fuzzy Pattern Trees (FPT) are generated and utilized for fastening classification of IoT malwares and enhancing detection accuracy.

In chapter 4, an experimental evaluation of the above mentioned schemes was achieved by performing various analyses by comparing the proposed scheme with the existing schemes and the results obtained possess with higher accuracy rate of 98% in overall, precision with 96%, and recall with 95% and active specificity with 98%.

Finally, chapter 5 concludes this thesis and future scope of the research in context to the proposed methodologies is also detailed.

1.4 SUMMARY

IoT security is one of the most important security feature necessary in day to day life, as the life getting heavily dependent on IoT based things. The main advantage and disadvantage of IoT based smart home appliances and device is that they are connected to the internet. In the advantage sense it makes the life easy and comfortable. The disadvantage is that the hackers can easily hack and gain access over the IoT based appliances and devices. So the IoT security provides a security for IoT based devices and appliances. IoT security is much needed because from increasing the safety of roads, cars, and homes, to fundamentally improving the way the manufacture and consumer products, IoT solutions provide valuable data and insights that will enhance the way the work and live.

The success depends on ensuring the integrity and confidentiality of IoT solutions and data while mitigating cybersecurity risks. The below are the serious risks involved in IoT solutions.

No physical boundaries: IoT devices transcend the traditional network perimeter and exist out there in the open. Traditional security approaches to restrict access to the devices are no more applicable. These devices can be shifted to any new location as and when needed and can be configured to access the network.

Weak password protection: The password used by people for their IoT devices are too easy to crack. As people, use the IoT devices or appliances for their comfort only.

Lack of regular patch updates: Many companies or the service providers don't bother about updating their devices in future, so they don't release the software updates regularly and by doing so the IoT device's vulnerabilities increases.

Remote exposures: Unlike other technologies, IoT devices have a particularly large attack surface due to their internet-supported connectivity. While, this accessibility is extremely valuable, it also grants hackers the opportunity to interact with devices remotely.This is why hacking campaigns like phishing are particularly effective. IoT security, like cloud security, has to account for a large number of entry points in order to protect assets. Access control: Many IoT devices do not comes with the access control mechanism for the user. Because of this, anybody can get into the system and can see the user's details.

Lack of device management: People purchase IoT devices for their comfort and leave them stick to or placed somewhere that can be accessed by any outsider or unethical individual. Physical possession of the device: This is perhaps the worst of all the threat vectors where attackers gain physical access to devices and workloads. With this kind of access, attackers can easily get to the internals of devices and their content, but with tools like Bus Pirate, Shikra or Logic Analyzers, they can read all communication flowing in the network as well. Through physical possession of an IoT device, an attacker can extract cryptographic secrets, modify its programming or replace with another device under their control. Hence, there is a need for a strong security framework in IoT.

CHAPTER 2

LITERATURE SURVEY

In this thesis, the comprehensive survey on the state of the art techniques in Internet of Things (IoT) security is discussed. Further, this chapter also discusses about the various schemes used in IoT security, process and procedures.

Cloud deployment reached high development rate in the prediction period of IoT security market. It mainly contributes towards cost reduction of enterprises in software, hardware, storage and technical force. Cloud platforms ensure security solutions for small scale and medium scale enterprises with limited budgets and investments. In addition, cloud deployment model is simple for maintaining and upgrading. Smart home and consumer electronics fields are anticipated with privileged development rate. Smart home is the result of integrating IoT facilitated living by ensuring security and comfort. Devices related to various body wears and smart home appliances are included for developing smart home and consumer electronics devices which lead to much number of security vulnerabilities and exploitations. Likewise IoT market space, North America holds maximum market space for IoT security too universally. Further, most number of cyber-attack cases are reported in North America worldwide. It is observed as largest and superior in adopting IT security and infrastructure. Even several governments are also focusing in integrating with industries for improved IoT security environment.

IoT Literature Survey

The author takes an objective of IoT level security to defend the attacker and to maintain the privacy, integrity, availability and confidentiality of the user data, network infrastructure, and physical device of IoT. This work analyzes the various IoT security level from 2016 to 2018, its current issues. This work gives an overview of current problems and solutions to the researchers with respect to the already available tools, IoT modelers and other simulators to find the attack scenario on the IoT devices (Hassan & Wan Haslina 2019).

The author presents a roadmap of IoT security based on the systemic and proposed cognitive approach along with the real time case study. The case study includes the highlights of individual components and interactions of systemic and novel cognitive approach which includes the security of privacy, identification, trust of device and privilege control access. Author proposes the different type of classification with respect to IoT vision and its security issues. The taxonomy of IoT security addresses the different challenges to researchers that are highlighted and the various solutions to research activities to protect the IoT devices from the attacker (Sfar *et al.,* 2018).

Author proposed a very attractive and unique solution for IoT management issues for large scale multi - technological network. To address these challenges in IoT, author presented a novel method called Software-Defined Networks (SDNs) in collaboration with IoT (SDN-IoT) which is an attractive solution but it is a heterogeneous in upcoming days of IoT systems. Due to multi-technology network, nodes present in the networks are heterogeneity in SDN-IoT, that may affect the control flow of the data or the application specific QoS. Likewise, the QoS highly influences in terms of security adopted within the network of IoT nodes. Both QoS and security factors are interdependent, but the network interconnected to IoT nodes are heterogeneity. So, these factors cannot be avoided during the connection establishment within the IoT network. Based on this, author gives a two-stage solution for addressing the above solution (Sood, K *et al.,* 2020).

The Machine Learning (ML) and Deep Learning (DL) are more preferable for last few years in various applications. Now, these algorithms are more popular in the field of security of various domains mostly in IoT systems to secure the data communication between the devices/nodes. The aim of the author is to explain the deep analysis of both ML/DL that can be used to improve the security in terms of data authentication and integrity of the device between the users present in the available network on the IoT systems. The authors present the various attacks on IoT security and its possible threats on the attacks. Finally, the advantages, challenges, opportunities and possible outcomes of each ML/DL were explained (Al-Garadi, MA *et al.,* 2020).

Author highlights the IoT communication issues and solutions at protocol level because of the currently available internet architecture. Now a day's the entire internet are working at IP-based communication protocols that plays a vital role to connect the possible servers to collect the data and transfer to the users. During the communication, some factors like power efficiency at the time of data exchange, reliability of data and usage of the internet to connect the device are most constrain elements in IoT system architecture. To protect these factors, the security is the major thing of all the IoT applications as well as various research issues (Granjal, J *et al.,* 2015).

In organization, security researchers are proved that most of the IoT devices are hacked by the attackers. In daily life most of the used devices belongs to IoT, apart from day-to-day life these devices are widely spread across all the areas. Detecting a malicious activity in IoT device connected in a same network is a very crucial task for the security people. The entire devices connected in networks are not included in a "White List" of trustworthy of device that should be detected. Author used Random Forest based Supervised Machine Learning (ML) algorithm which was applied on the collected features from a network data to classify the IoT device from the White List. By training the features and evaluate multi-class classifiers, the data from a collected network and labeled data were classified from 17 distinct data, it represents 9 types of devices.

The analysis is based on the unauthorized IoT device which was correctly detected by unknown in 96% of test cases followed by white listed device which were correctly detected by their actual device in 99% of case. By this analysis, author claimed that some of the IoT devices are detected quickly when compared to other devices like socket and thermostats that were detected within five TCP sessions (Meidan, Y *et al.,* 2017). The perfect detection of unauthorized IoT device of this machine learning method gives an accuracy of 99.49% with 346 consecutive sessions.

In addition, the author (Iqbal, H *et al.,* 2020) explains the various threats, security premises, attack vectors based on IoT networks. The communication of data from one node to another via the network-based architecture deployment through Software-Define Network (SDN) is proposed by the author.

This work presents a SDN based deployment model on IoT network (centralized and decentralized). J.Jeon et al (Jeon, J *et al.,* 2020), proposed a dynamic based malware analysis at IoT device (DAIMD) to reduce the damages to the entire IoT device connected to the network by detecting the known and unknown malwares of different variants involved intelligently. This is a Convolution Neural Network (CNN) deep learning model to detect and analyze the malwares on IoT dynamically in an open environment. This is a best method to detect a malware dynamically in a cloud environment to analysis the behavior of malwares related to the memory, network, and

Physical file system, process of data and system call functions. After the features are extracted and converted, the behavioral data into image to classify the malware and trained the system using CNN. This model predicts the new malwares very effectively on the IoT devices.

The deep learning based intrusion detection work is carried out by I.Ullah (Ullah & Mahmoud, QH 2021), uses the convolution neural network based anomaly-based intrusion detection model for predicting the IoT nodes present in the network. Author proposed a CNN model first to create a multiclass classification with 1D, 2D and 3D. This model is validating using various detection datasets like BoT-IoT, IoT intrusion Networks, MQTT-IoT-IDS2020 and IoT-23 Intrusion which are recent attacks datasets to perform the analysis. Binary implement is done by a transfer learning method and the pre-trained model run on multiclass classification of CNN. Both binary and multiclass classification model gives the better results in terms of accuracy, precision, recall and F1 score compared with the existing deep learning algorithms like CNN, C-CMU, C-LSTM-AE etc.

Pradeep Sudhakaran *et al.,* [10] on this particular the IoT gadgets malware were detected using the deep learning techniques. The investigation is carried out by the freely available datasets on Ember Opcode which utilizes the malicious and original documents (out of 70,140 subsets, 69,860 are victim documents). This model gives the better results for detecting the IoT gadgets like cameras, smoke detectors, sensible thermostats, and sensible light-weight bulbs and so on using deep learning algorithms.

This work reveals the detailed survey on recent security attacks and its privacy challenges related to the IoT layered architecture. The perception, network and application layer are the major categories involved in the IoT systems. Author claims that block chain technology is one of the key factors to protect the IoT security and privacy of the IoT architecture. Block chain and its added factors which are combined with other new methods as ML to avoid the intrusion detection on the network or a system. This survey is based on 4-tier architecture layer to identify the vulnerabilities on security level and privacy to mitigate the risk through Block chain technology [https://www.marketsandmarkets.com].

Physical Attacks

In physical attacks, attacker utilizes hardware part of the IoT device. Various kinds of physical attacks are implemented which are network disruption, physical impair, malware injection and object jamming (https://www.marketsandmarkets.com-https://cybersecurity.att.com). By these attacks, components of devices are damaged and their functions are interrupted. During malware injection, attacker affects the targeted device by injecting virus by making use of USB. Signals are blocked and manipulated by equipping signal jammers by the attackers (Akram, H *et al.,* 2018). Permanent Denial of Service (PDoS) attacks targets IoT device with high voltage power supply and it maximizes the load and insist for alteration (https://www.trgdatacenters.com).

Attackers discover various ways to target IoT devices from several distinct attack vectors because of not maintaining high standards. Attack vector will differ amid various IoT devices by considering three primary factors like hardware and software configurations of IoT device, connected network and associated application. Several kinds of attacks are related with IoT securities which are physical attacks, Man in the Middle (MITM) attack, Bluetooth Man in the Middle attack, Invalid data injection attack, BoT nets and Denial of Service attacks.

During initial reconnaissance, attackers observe IoT devices consistently to discover vulnerabilities for implementing attack. Duplicate IoT device is utilized in which reverse engineering is applied by creating experimental attack and outcomes are observed carefully. Internal hardware system is analyzed for examining software and corrupting microcontrollers in order to discover the confidential information. Hardware related security provides solutions for facing reverse engineering and ensures device authentication mechanisms. Sensors, actuators, connectivity and power supply are included in application processor and it is located in damages resisting environment.

Man-in-the-Middle (MITM) Attack

MITM attack is the most familiar attack which interrupts communication amid nodes and permits to act as proxy by taking control. Most of the MITM attacks are launched amid client / server and attackers. In IoT ecosystem, MITM attack is implemented between device and related application. Lack of standards of IoT devices lead to MITM attacks. Cloud polling and direct connections are two general methods of MITM attack. Firmware updates are observed during cloud polling where stable communication is carried between smart home device and cloud. Address Resolution Protocol (ARP) poisoning is performed to change the Domain Name System (DNS) in order to redirect the traffic of network or disrupt HTTPS traffic making use of self-signed certificates or tools like strip Secure Sockets Layer (SSL) (https://www.globalsign.com). Legitimacy or trust intensity is not verified by most of the IoT devices. During direct connection method, devices perform communication via hub or application of similar network. Attacker can identify IoT devices over network by snooping IP address of exact port. Smart refrigerator shows the Google calendar of customer and that can be affected by MITM IoT attack. SSL certificate validation is performed here which makes ease attacker to obtain Google credentials by launching MITM attack.

Several MITM IoT attacks are implemented through Bluetooth. Bluetooth Low Energy (BLE) is used for executing and designing several IoT devices by considering the features such as compact, least cost and energy efficient (Melamed, T 2018). But BLE is targeted by MITM attacks. AES-CCM encryption algorithm is utilized by BLE to ensure security but encryption key sharing is not in secured manner. Security level of temporary key sharing is based on pairing method amid devices. BLE has three stages of pairing process. At first stage, pairing request is sent by the initiating device which is occurred through insecure channel.

Temporary keys are exchanged and verified in second stage and then one short term key is generated by making use of Elliptic Curve Diffie-Hellman public-key cryptography. At final stage, generated key is shared in secured channel which is used to perform data encryption. Pairing method plays major role in identifying temporary key on the basis of OS level. While considering with IoT, there are 3 general pairing methods which are Just Works, Passkey and Out-of-Band pairing method. During Just Works method, temporary key is set as 0 and it is insecure. In Passkey method, combination of 6 digit number is used and that should be entered by the user which is considered as fairly secure and it is possible to bypass them. Temporary key are exchanged in Out-of-Band pairing method by making use of Near Field Communication like methods. Security capacities of exchange method define the security level of this method. Protected exchange channel without MITM attacks leads to protected BLE connection. Out-of-Band method is not familiar for IoT devices.

Profiling based Schemes

Additional feature of BLE devices are considered as Generic Attribute Profile (GATT) and standardized data schema is used for device communication. Roles of devices, general behaviors and Meta data are described by GATT. GATT schema can be read by BLE application of an IoT device within certain range. With 2 connected BLE devices, it is possible to implement MITM attacks in network where one device acts as connected IoT device while targeting mobile app. GATTacker kind of tools are available for BLE MITM attacks implementation.

If an IoT device with the implementation of MITM attack, then it is possible for False Data Injection (FDI) attack (Ahmed, M & Pathan, ASK 2020). Sensor data can be altered by FDI attacks and imperfect output data will be obtained at the end. There are various ways for FDI attacks implementation whereas MITM attack based is more familiar. FDI attacks compromise sensor data and predictive maintenance systems algorithm which is generally used for monitoring machine status and predict time of maintenance. Predictive maintenance algorithms are utilized for smart cities. FDI attacks are dangerous to power systems which will affect the states of power grid and distribution process.

Denial of Service (DoS) Attacks

DDoS attacks are targeted against IoT devices to make them as vulnerable and PDoS attacks make devices as inoperable entirely. It will be achieved by implementing firmware attacks where power system is overloaded. Firmware attack tries to corrupt OS or faulty version of software (https://www.trgdatacenters.com). If this process is implemented legally, then it is referred as flashing and illegal implementation is defined as phlashing. If a device is phlashed, that device should be flashed to get clear OS replica. Recovery is not possible during powerful attack implementation. Malware injected USB device can completely impair the system or device is an example for this attack. BrickerBot is example for PDoS malware which implements brute force dictionary attacks for getting IoT devices permissions and once it's executed then it will impair the complete system.

Misconfiguration of storage & kernel, delayed internet connection, device performance disruption and cleaning all device files are performed by these commands (http://www.trend micro .com). Various attack vectors are available in IoT ecosystem because of its structure. Mostly weak links related to connection of IoT devices are targeted by the attackers. Strong protection mechanism is mandatory nowadays to combat against such kinds of attacks and high security standards should be maintained to ensure user in secured environment. Countermeasures should be considered to resolve the caused damages after the implementation of attacks.

Most of the security experts and analysts turned into AI for real time protection against cyber threats and vulnerabilities. Utilization AI is more familiar in developing intrusion detection system in order to combat against cyber security attacks by performing traffic pattern analysis and observing properties of attack. Security is a severe issue for IoT, big data and artificial intelligence. Increased amount of smart devices creates demands in understanding newly arriving IoT security threats to build secured approach to combat against attacks. Several IoT vulnerabilities are available related to network, software, and hardware and chip level.

Considering network vulnerability, secured end node connection of IoT network will create effective and fast communication amidst them. Attack vectors will be created by the adversary people by acquiring every loophole in order to reveal confidential information. Recently, attackers compromised Amazon IoT devices like home security camera and ring doorbell (Stone, J 2019). Attackers gained access of IoT devices by intercepting the usernames and passwords via an unencrypted HyperText Transfer Protocol (HTTP) of host network. There are possibilities for breaching IoT security camera and speech assistants like Google home and Alexa in simple manner (Lei, X *et al.,* 2018). Most of the IoT devices are based on UPnP protocols which are integrated with the features like simple configuration and control. But, HTTP protocol is used by UPnP and there is no assurance for secret and reliable protection and it is possible to impair UPnP protocol because of its lack in validation, authentication and logging. Smart home environment is not safe if it is not implemented with appropriate protection mechanism.

Malware based Attacks

Attackers control the functionalities of IoT devices via software vulnerabilities. IoT devices are under attack while they are incorporated with insecure configurations and fragile authentication mechanisms (Rodrigues, B 2015). Third party applications damage security of IoT smart home (Fernandes, E *et al.,* 2017). Malwares lead cyber-attacks superiorly and information of targeted device is leaked and then usual function flow is disrupted. IoT monitoring system is employed for automating smart grid system. Real time information is collected for monitoring control plants and their status. Still, few of them are not running with updated versions of operating systems like Windows 10 and they are executed with Windows XP or Windows 7. Host firewall is not available in older versions of OS and attackers target them by implementing worm attacks (Stoffer, V 2013). If the office network is collapsed, then connected server will also be affected which will result complete shutdown. Russian Gas Company is attacked in 2000 by making use of Trojan virus where gas pipeline's control is lost. Attacker can launch any kind of attack once data collection is completed by Trojan. Software vulnerabilities permit to access and control IoT devices and environment. Firmware's are dangerous which will affect regular operations.

Real time data attainment is performed by IoT sensors remotely for reducing network load. In power generation plants, such sensors are implanted and they observe the demand of load and manage generator's turbine (Kayastha, N *et al.,* 2014). Several sensors are with minimal energy and encrypted data transmission is implemented. Man in the Middle Attack (MITM) is performed by the attacker to reveal confidential information or signal manipulation. Attackers generate new entry points during attacks based on Advanced smart Metering Infrastructure (AMI) for breaching network information. Along with data theft, power theft and power related issues are primarily aimed by attackers. Further, spoofing attacks are implemented over Industrial, Scientific Medical band (ISM band) where several devices struggle for utilizing spectrum. Masquerade attack is also possible during data propagation. Attacker will interfere smart meters via replay attack where he could send invalid measurement to the legitimate users.

Hardware Trojan in IoT devices

Hardware Trojan (HT) payloads are injected in the available circuit which changes the functions once activated. System security bypass is intended by the attackers for performing information leak. Digital and analog HT payload vulnerabilities target towards integrate chip like application-specific system-on-chip and field-programmable gate array devices. As IoT is adopted with minimal power feature it is found that cryptographic units are in unsecured manner. Hardware vulnerabilities like HTs are more dangerous than software bugs which are unable to remove easily and demand more cost for removal. HT will permanently impair the system and ruins services.

HTs are simply executed by third party untrusted IP vendors. Side channel electromagnetic analysis is performed for observing the behaviors of IoT devices (Spreitzer, R *et al.,* 2018). Side channel attacks aims to obtain the secret key of IoT device. Encrypted key information is extracted as a crypto block module during side channel attack. Guessing passwords and key information is possible by computing power consumption and cryptographic operations based electromagnetic emissions. For decrypting significant information, attackers analyze side channel information like voltage, current, thermal radiations and time related information. Cryptographic algorithm AES-128 is intercepted and secret key is obtained by implementing Correlation Electromagnetic Analysis attack. Further, it is found that 4096 bit RSA decryption key can be extracted by making use of sensitive micro phone located 4m distance from IoT device.

Several IoT based security vulnerability incidents are reported. Massive development and insufficient security features increased eagerness of attackers to break or impair the entire IoT ecosystem. Denial of Service (DoS) attack is implemented in several well - known websites such as Twitter and GitHub by compromising interconnected domain name providers of IoT network. AT &T Alien labs identified Botenago malware in November, 2021. It targeted above one million devices as well as routers and more than 30 distinct exploitations are identified (https://www.cloudflare.com). It is based on Golang which is an open source programming language of Google. While targeting attacks, backdoor is created and port number 19412 is utilized.

Botnets

Botnets are more familiar in the implementation of attacks against IoT devices. Many devices are employed to build botnets in order to launch DDoS attacks. DDoS attack ruins legitimacy of services and it is achieved by using many components. Flow of data is disrupted and it aims to collapse infrastructure. Recruitment, exploitation and infection and attack are some phases of a general DDoS attack. During recruitment phase, vulnerable machines are scanned to identify target. By injecting malicious codes, vulnerable machines are broken during exploitation and infection phase. Further, attacker examines those affected machines and schedules for attack. In attack phase, infectious machines are taken control by attacker for forwarding malicious packets against target. Getting infected machines and implementing DDoS attacks via IoT devices is one of the familiar ways because of lack in security maintenance.

Mirai worm is the most familiar malware which performed biggest DDoS attacks and its design is intended to compromise and take control over the IoT devices like CCTV cameras, DVRs, and home routers [26]. Infected IoT devices acts and contributes majorly for large-scale botnet and implies various types of DDoS attacks. Mirai targets many distinct familiar CPU architectures of IoT devices like ARM, x86, PowerPC, Sparc and Motorola to seize maximum amount of devices. Mirai virus is with compact size and it does not exist in hard disk of the devices but staying in memory and virus is vanished while rebooting the device. Infected devices are vulnerable to reinfection and it will take few minutes.

Okiru, Satori and Reaper are few familiar IoT botnet viruses resulted from the source code of Mirai. Mirai botnet is one of hazardous one for IoT ecosystem which utilizes default usernames and passwords for targeting several connected devices. Internet of IoT devices is scanned initially. Internet Connected Autonomous Vehicles (CAVs) are compromised and controlled by Mirai botnet. Mirai botnet causes infection to smart devices which are executing over ARC processors by launching DDoS attacks. 40% of the malware assault cases are registered because of Mirai. It is created by kids to carry online services on the basis of DDoS attacks. IoT devices and Command and Control (C&C), severs are infected by applying self-replication technique. In addition, Trojans are also employed for Mirai botnet development. Mostly, Industrial IoT got affected by advanced Mirai malwares.

IoT technologies are incorporated in several real time application areas like healthcare systems, smart homes, smart cities and surveillance. Strengthened authentication mechanisms are needed for implementing secured IoT environment. Light weighted smart devices are developed with minimal memory capacity and energy consumption. Further, security based attack vectors are defined by transforming computational boundaries.

IoT reference model with seven layers is introduced in 2014 by Intel, IBM and Cisco in IoT world forum for educating the people of development and research community (cdn.iotwf.com). Physical devices and controllers, Connectivity, Edge computing, Data accumulation, Data abstraction, Application and Collaboration and Process are the seven layers of IoT reference model. Physical layer includes sensors, devices, machines and intelligent nodes. Connectivity layer is implemented with communication and processing units. Edge computing layer performs data element analysis and transformation. Data accumulation layer is mainly meant for storage purpose of IoT network. Data abstraction layer involves in aggregation and accessing. Application layer provides the operations like reporting, analytic and control of IoT environment. Finally, collaboration and process layer involves the processes related to people and processes. Various types of sensor applications are included in physical layer which are wireless sensors, embedded sensors and USB. Main function of sensor is data collection which includes environmental data like pressure, temperature, gas, temperature and optical measurement.

Internet connectivity provides enhanced and effective data transfer amid the end systems within the network and IoT business market is enlarged with maximized progress over the decade. Consumer electronics sector earned huge income flow and significant growth because of increased connectivity. IoT integrated smart home appliances provide simple, effective and safeguard environment. Smart home system is set with the help of embedded sensors, actuators and additional computing devices.

Several industrial autonomous sectors are equipped with IoT applications. For example, in Amazon warehouse, robots are used for goods transport and management. Human intervention is avoided inside the warehouse while robots roaming inside. They are communicated via wireless technologies like Zigbee, Bluetooth and so on. But security and privacy breaches are appeared among IoT applications and devices.

Zigbee is IEEE 802.15.4 based wireless protocol and it has network and application layer based stack profile. As Zigbee security keys are symmetric and there are possibilities to compromise them to obtain the sensitive information by performing network vulnerability towards IoT devices (Farahani, S 2008). Even while using Zigbee Light Link based connected network attackers will disclose confidential information (Morgner, P *et al.,* 2016). Pre-defined keys sharing leads to insecure key management and public key frameworks should be ignored for effective key management system. Further, limited energy consumption policies of IoT devices also affect key management system.

Light weighted key authentication schemes are inadequate for large scaled organizations. IPv4 and IPv6 are two familiar remote accessing network protocols. It is possible to access IoT devices remotely through Telnet like command line interfaces. As IoT ecosystem is dealt with consistent wide range data flow, massive network traffic loss can occur due to data loss or Denial of Service (DoS) attack. Hidden malwares in IoT devices can generate IoT botnets by launching DDoS attacks (Angrishi, K 2017).

Power grid system of Austria and German are malfunctioned in 2013 by implementing self-inflicted DDoS flooding attack. IoT network, devices and protocols are collapsed for the moment of DDoS attack. Automated smart grid system is mainly based on IoT monitoring. Real time data is collected by sensors to observe the conditions of control plants and their apparatus. While attack is implemented, plant functionalities will be collapsed without monitoring. Even nuclear power plant can be affected by any malware or spyware.

Mostly confidential information is shared by IoT devices through core controllers. Programmable Logic Controllers (PLCs) are targeted for Stuxnet malware attack to enable machine process automation (Langner, R 2011). Stuxnet infects the targeted plant via USB. When the control system is infected, network operations are spied to collect information. Plant's control module is seized after collecting appropriate data and then attack is launched to impair plant operation. It is primarily developed by aiming Iran's nuclear facilities (i.e. Uranium Enrichment Plant) however, it is altered and implemented in other energy generative facilities. It creates more interest for media in 2010 because it is reported as first case for computer worm in impairing the hardware.

Based on McKinsey Global Institute's prediction report, worldwide 64 million IoT devices will be used in the year 2025 i.e 127 newly connected devices will be available per second (Petrov, C 2019)- (Azmoodeh, A *et al.,* 2018). Mass utilization of IoT devices will direct towards large scaled attacks today (Sakhnini, J *et al.,* 2019). To avoid exploitations and their crucial impacts, it is mandatory to combat powerfully. Implementation of IoT security mechanisms should be advanced effectively by overcoming the shortcoming of the traditional systems and considering the advanced methods and techniques of new generation malwares or security breaches. Proper security metrics should be considered for IoT interconnected devices in order to battle against various attacks with the consideration of issues of security, confidentiality and privacy and the following concerns.

- All equipped devices in IoT ecosystem need to be switched on all time and it makes simple for attackers to examine device's power mode every time. As IoT is a set of interconnected devices and equipment's, attackers are allowed to access them.

- Poor encryption features and weak security procedures of interconnected devices are the reasons for IoT malwares and their damages towards IoT ecosystem.

- Further each and every interconnected device need internet all time and it permits attackers involving vulnerable IoT attacks.

On the basis of SonicWall, size of IoT malware attacks is 32.4 million in 2020 which is inflated by 30% (https://www.sonicwall.com). Mostly IoT devices like voice-control smart devices, door bells, TV camera and other apparatuses are lack in security which makes ease attackers with various accessing entries. An unanticipated IoT device flooding in networks increased the threat rate proportionally during the consecutive COVID - 19 pandemic periods.

Linux based IoT malware Kaiji is discovered in 2020 which is completely developed using Golang by launching brute force attacks in Secure Shell (SSH). It gets root access to a device and spreads to further devices by discovering the unsecured SSH ports of Linux servers and IoT devices over internet (Vasan, D *et al.,* 2020). At last C&C server commands are fetched for performing DDoS attack. Further, several attacks are launched like SYN flood, TCP, UDP, ACK flood attack and IP spoofing [89-90]. Muhstik botnet is discovered in the starting of 2020 by Palo Alto Networks which applies authentication related brute force attacks in the routers (such as tomato router, GPON home router and DD-WRT router) which infects cloud servers. It is based on the services related to XMRig, cgmining and DDoS attack. Various web application exploitations are applied for infecting cloud servers (Jeon, J *et al.,* 2020).

Mukashi Mirai is identified by Palo Alto Networks which is novel variant of Mirai. It targeted Network-Attached Storage (NAS) devices which permits attackers to operate their malicious codes remotely against infected system. It is based on brute force attack and aims to deal with C&C server. In addition through this malware, it is possible to compromise system security, violate user privacy and perform information theft by making use of backdoor commands. These attacks are most dangerous and they are developed with the intension of impairing devices and IoT ecosystem. Security researchers suggest security systems with multi -factor authentication for evading and battling against attackers.

As IoT ecosystem is vast with enormous amount of data, such mass data requires appropriate analysis (Jia, Y *et al.,* 2020 - Ghahramani, M *et al.,* 2021, Xenofontos, C *et al.,* 2022). To accomplish that, Artificial Intelligence (AI) and Machine Learning (ML) are incorporated to increase the potential of IoT ecosystem. In recent, AI-based Intrusion Detection Systems (AI-IDS) is utilized for continuous network investigation, earlier attack related information collection and analysis. AI-IDS combat against threats by predicting attack on the basis of historical data (Dib, M *et al.,* 2021 - Torabi, S *et al.,* 2021, Dinakarrao). Modern techniques are advanced based on the approaches adapted by the attackers. ML algorithms such as Linear Discriminant Analysis (LDA), Random Forest (RF) and Classification and Regression Trees (CART) are applied to resolve the real time attack prediction and categorization (Mazhar, N *et al.,* 2021).

There are two kinds of ML based IDS which are Anomaly based IDS and Signature based IDS. Anomaly based IDS discovers attacks on the basis of already available normal behavior in which comparison is done among the current and previous real time traffics (Ravi, N & Shalinie, SM 2020) (Sathyadevan, S *et al.,* 2019) . Signature based IDS evaluates the familiar patterns of real time traffic and known patterns of earlier attacks. Machine learning contributes more in cyber security field and several ML algorithms are utilized such as Decision trees, naïve Bayes, k-nearest neighbor, support vector machines, artificial neural networks and so on (Liu, Y *et al.,* 2020). Supervised learning and unsupervised learning are two kinds of machine learning. Training data is manually labeled with the classes of malware or benign by making use of algorithms in supervised learning. Data coherence and data modularity amid classes are considered instead of algorithms in unsupervised learning (Agiollo, A *et al.,* 2021).

In decision tree, training data is involved to iterative division process by applying set of optimized rules to classify either attack or normal (Mohammed, H *et al.,* 2020, Mishra, N & Pandya, S 2021, Khan, AY *et al.,* 2020, Hussain, F *et al.,* 2020, Das, AK *et al.,* 2021, Zhang, N *et al.,* 2019, Doshi, K *et al.,* 2021). Command injection attacks of robotic vehicles are detected by classifying values like network flow, CPU utilization and data volume. Euclidean distance method is employed in KNN based learning phase of data samples. To learn novel traffic patterns quickly, IDS utilize KNN approach mostly. It will help to perform real time cyber-attack detection (Meneghello, F et al., 2019). SVMs are extended versions of linear regression models where plane is placed to divide data samples as two distinct classes and the plane can vary based on function of algorithm like polynomial, linear, non - linear, sigmoid, Gaussian and so on. Internet traffic patterns are analyzed and categorized using SVMs as classes of HTTP, FTP, SMTP, etc. ANN is similar to brain neuron of human system which is implemented for cyber-attack security. ANN mathematical models are formed in order to focus on new kinds of traffic and attacks (Lounis, K & Zulkernine 2020) (Neshenko, N *et al.,* 2019).

Attackers are also utilizing AI to evade from IDS algorithms and implementing as malicious. ML is used by attackers for vulnerability exploitation against targeted system (Sharma, V *et al.,* 2020, Wang, J 2021, Lins, FAA & Vieira, M 2021). IoT devices with low security standards are concentrated and AI is utilized for discovering device vulnerabilities whereas zero day vulnerabilities are also implemented. Developers should fix each and every vulnerability by considering the smartness of attackers in exploiting vulnerabilities. Familiar techniques like fuzzing and symbolic execution are applied for vulnerability detection in automated manner (Rana, MM & Bo, R 2019).

Random inputs are generated while utilizing fuzzing which is referred as testing technique. Inputs can be in any formats such as binary, numbers, chars, known to dangerous values, meta data, special characters and SQL requests (Jurn J et al.,) (Shafiq, M et al., 2021). Dumb fuzzing and smart fuzzing are the types of fuzzing. Input variables are randomly changed to create defects by dumb fuzzing and it seems as fast and simple but its performance is poor. On the basis of software's format and error generation, smart fuzzing creates input values. Expert knowledge and tuning is required for effective smart fuzzing (Nasralla, MM *et al.,* 2020).

Symbolic execution is another method of fuzzing where, vulnerabilities search is implemented by considering input variables as symbol not value. It is divided as offline and online symbolic execution (Raoof, A *et al.,* 2019). Offline symbolic execution selects single path only for exploration within the time which avoids algorithm's execution from starting and overcomes the burden of code re-execution. Online symbolic execution duplicates states and path prediction is done at every branch statement. Overhead is minimum during online symbolic execution however huge memory is required for processing (Yang, N *et al.,* 2021, Dushku, E *et al.,* 2020, Hossain, M & Xie, J

2020, Ravi, N & Shalinie, SM 2020). If the attacker malfunction AI system by making use of invalid input then it is considered as input attack. Attack patterns are added during input attack by the attackers. For example, if minimal noise is added to the images of smart driving cars then it will confuse the system and human itself (https://www.f5.com).

Altering input is enough to compromise output for input attack and there is no need to compromise algorithm and security of AI system (George, G & Thampi, SM 2018, Khanam, S *et al.,* 2020, Hassija, V *et al.,* 2019). Minimal change will direct to wrong execution of algorithm and complicated attacks are hidden in nature. After implementing input attacks successfully attackers simply perform data poisoning attack, algorithm poisoning attack, dataset poisoning attack and model poisoning which is considered as highly dangerous. While AI is used for detecting aircraft implemented data poisoning attack will advantageous for enemy they will able to identify them and alter their directions (Hussain, F *et al,* 2021, Sudheera, KLK et al., 2021). Dataset poisoning is the straightway of data poisoning which will help to acquire entire knowledge of datasets. Poisoned datasets damage the process of discovering pattern and will misguide AI in wrong way. For large scaled dataset, discovering poisoned dataset is a challengeable task. Algorithm poisoning attack will lead to attain confidential information for the attackers. The poisoned algorithm will compromise other algorithms and also the model. It is based on federated learning. Attackers aim to swap legitimate model with poisoned model by implementing model poisoning attack which is hazardous for the entire system (Bhayo, J *et al.,* 2020, Makhdoom, I *et al.,* 2019).

Summary

Few technologies are integrated together inevitably. IoT and AI are appropriate example for such amalgamation of technologies. World of IoT is growing superfast and vast of connected devices which require proper analytics approaches. Rapid decision making should be implemented by utilizing enormous amount of IoT data.

AI provides improved analytics to increase market value of IoT. AI with Deep learning or Machine learning influence IoT business and useful for predicting the forthcoming needs of customers and IoT ecosystem. Preventive actions are required for automotive system implementation on the basis of behavioral analysis conducted in services and products. Autonomous systems are providing better results in decision making process for smart industries, smart cities and smart homes. Physical world is digitized by IoT sensors and data is obtained in various formats like video, audio, RFID data and so on. Processing of raw data or structured data requires implemented models of edge, ML and DL. Today HD cameras are utilized for smart city like projects and sensors should meet the requirements by segregating noise data from appropriate data. In addition data with various velocities should be fixed with exact environment. In some exceptional cases historical data should be involved for enhancing decision making in effective manner. Data fusion is performed in order to attain better results while data is obtained from several layers and formats. ML and DL tools are utilized for real time data fusion from different layers along with capturing data. Further optimized resource processing is implemented by AI and ML analytics.

AI and ML integrated IoT applications and devices grasps productivity, effectiveness and efficiency is gaining successful transformation of raw data as actions. It resolves the shortcomings related big data like massive environment and provides improved decision making after data processing. AI and ML amalgamation increases the accuracy, efficiency, productivity and cost effectiveness. Further, it improvised communication and real time computation of IoT environment. Accessibility and IoT data analysis are found as general challenges for enterprises. Statistical analysis is implemented making use of AI and ML which presents proactive and preventive actions to resolve those issues. AI enabled IoT systems provides automated and consistent solutions.

While considering attack mitigation inputs sanitization is recommend along with abnormal data checking. Some attacks are dif.ficult to recognize by AI due to development of malicious AI systems. Several researchers are working on AI based security systems due to the exhaustive resource of AI and high-level knowledge based familiar algorithms. In such a way, attackers find difficult in accessing and maintaining AI based security systems. To ensure the IoT ecosystem, devices, network and applications in secured manner by avoiding threats, attacks and vulnerabilities the following conditions need to be considered.

- ***Secured IoT network***: IoT network need to be secured and protected during internet connection by implementing conventional security mechanism like firewalls, anti-virus, anti-malware protection mechanisms and Intrusion Detection and Prevention System (IDPS).

- ***IoT devices authentication:*** User should permitted to authenticate their devices making use of various management features for an IoT device and robust authentication approaches are required such as multi factor authentication, bio metrics and digital signatures.

- ***Unique identification:*** It will help trace IoT devices if their behavior is abnormal or they are related with malicious devices.

- ***Secured Gateways:*** Secured gateways prevent attackers from accessing IoT devices. They act as interface amid IoT devices and network and they support for implementing strong security features by acting as a bridge.

- ***Updates and patches:*** Developers and manufacturers shall enable the process of updating software's automatically.

- ***Utilizing encrypted IoT data:*** User's privacy is protected and data breaches will be avoided while encrypting data communication amid end users by applying high standard cryptographic functions and algorithms. In addition usage of secured key lifecycle management processes will improve entire data security and privacy factors.

- ***Usage of PKI security methodologies:*** Secured connection is ensured in between IoT device and application can be achieved by using security methods of IoT Public Key Infrastructure like digital certificates (i.e. X.509), cryptographic key management, and life-cycle potentials comprised with creation, distribution, management and revocation of public or private key. PKI and digital certificates affords breach resistance for IoT devices and ecosystem.

- ***Security analytics utilization:*** IoT based attacks and intrusions can be identified by utilizing IoT security analytics and it will overcome the shortcomings related security issues of using firewalls.

- ***IoT API security methods utilization:*** Usage of IoT API security methods keep data integrity amid IoT end devices, back end and associated REST based applications. In addition device authorization is also ensured with the detection of attacks and threats of respective APIs. API security ensures secure data passage and authorization of IoT devices, applications and developers associated with APIs.

- ***IoT hardware testing:*** IoT hardware testing should be implemented in robust environment. It includes various factors such as capacity, range and latency. Hardware manufacturers must consider the processors with high level security and minimal power consumption. While incorporating with third party elements they need to be involved for complete testing and their proper functioning needed to ensure.

- ***Secured IoT applications development:*** IoT app developers should have deep and wide view in the aspect of IoT security. Complete study and research work should be carried before starting development.

- ***IoT security current trend awareness:*** Developers of IoT devices and applications should aware the current trend about the vulnerabilities and exploitations regarding to IoT ecosystem. In addition manufacturers also should have additional care to resolving the security breaches and attacks. Finally end users also have enough awareness and knowledge regarding threats, attacks and breaches of IoT.

- ***Implementation Challenges of proposed work:*** One of the most complex parts of IoT development is ensuring that the IoT application can be integrated with various platforms, OS, cloud services, and even legacy systems. The overall hardware requirements are not always aligned with the available resources, and it needs to be considered before the project is started. Devices that are not thoroughly tested can be a security threat, and often end up being unreliable. This increases the overheads and causes bottlenecks in the process, while also being a security issue.

- ***Privacy concerns of proposed IoT framework***

    - Misuse of Personal Information
    - Misinformation and Deep Fakes
    - Moral Use of Data and Resources

CHAPTER 3

METHODOLOGY

3.1 AN INTELLIGENT IoT ATTACK DETECTION FRAMEWORK USING EFFECTIVE EDGE AI BASED COMPUTING

3.1.1 Introduction

With the advanced growth of electronic communication technologies and IoT, our daily lifestyle is digitally connected (Hassan & Wan Haslina 2019). IoT plays a vital role in building smart world by allowing connections amid billions of smart devices and gadgets. Making use of advanced cyber technologies, it is possible to manage traditional systems in effective and efficient manner. Enormous amount of IoT applications are cultivated and installed recently which is aimed with much comfortable lifestyle. But risks are increased against physical systems in terms of cyber vulnerabilities and threats. Large amount of security vulnerability cases are reported today. As per Kaspersky IoT cyber-attacks are doubled in the first half of 2021 comparing to the previous year i.e 1.51 billion IoT breaches are happened which implies an increase as 639 million (Sfar *et al.,* 2018). Attacks like crypto currency mining, Distributed Denial of Service (DDoS) attacks played key roles in damaging the assets and stealing confidentiality of data (Granjal, J *et al.,* 2015) (Ullah & Mahmoud, QH 2021). Most of the attackers tried to get access in IoT networks through telnet protocol which is a command line interface used for enabling remote communication. Based on the results, pandemic worsened IoT vulnerabilities with the persistence of IoT device usage. Most of them seem weak because of their inadequate security protocols.

Security of IoT devices and its applications becomes one of the most substantial problems (https://www.f5.com). Injection of malicious code and security breaches will limit the development and deployment of IoT applications and will cause massive asset losses (Sood, K *et al.,* 2020). Providing sound security protection is a challengeable task for IoT applications along with resource limitations which seem main concerns (Al-Garadi, MA *et al.,* 2020). Multiple research works are carried for resolving the shortcomings of existing security methods (Ullah & Mahmoud, QH 2021) (https://cybersecurity.att.com)(Fernandes, E *et al.,* 2017). Modern security algorithms such as Attribute-Based Access Control (ABAC), group signature scheme, homomorphic encryption and asymmetric key related solutions are utilized and they require devices with appropriate computational power and memory for execution (Granjal, J *et al.,* 2015, Meidan, Y *et al.,* 2017). There are some issues while applying them in multiple IoT devices especially smart end devices.

Though cloud technologies provide enormous amount of resources, it could not able to meet the requirements for providing effective services for IoT end devices. To resolve such kind of issues edge computing technology is emerged for migrating the resources associated with computation and memory by forming an edge layer near IoT end device (Iqbal, H *et al.,* 2020). Thus, edge layer balances the loads of various tasks related to high level computation and resource on demand. This novel computing pattern simplifies resource management of IoT devices and also system performance is optimized (Jeon, J *et al.,* 2020, Ullah & Mahmoud, QH 2021, Sudhakaran & Pradeep 2021). In addition, it becomes as a new spot for developing and deploying IoT end devices in secured manner. Few researchers worked in the proposals related to IoT security solutions on the basis of edge computing which is included in various fields like security designs, firewalls, Intrusion Detection Systems (IDS), authentication and authorization protocols and privacy reserving methods (www.marketsandmarkets.com, www.cybersecurity.att.com, Akram et al., 2018, www. trgdatacenters. com, www.globalsign.com, Melamed, T 2018). Still researches related to IoT security on the basis of edge computing is in beginning stage. Comprehensive reviews to be done towards various refined edge computing based IoT security models.

The key contribution of the work are summarized as below:

- Edge computing based Intrusion/Attack Detection framework is proposed by utilizing the optimal selection algorithms in runtime based on the data input.
- Data interchange in IoT environment is secured by increasing speed of data processing by applying edge computing.
- Quality of Service (QoS) value is improved for effective communication with the integration of security essentials.

3.1.2 Related Work

Multiple research works are carried for protecting IoT end devices against various intrusion attacks like Man-In-The-Middle (MITM), Distributed Denial of Service (DDoS) and so on. Availability of data in IoT ecosystem is a main constraint where various decision making processes are depended on real time data (George, G & Thampi, SM 2018, Al-Garadi, MA *et al.,* 2020, Khanam, S *et al.,* 2020, Hassija, V *et al.,* 2019, Hussain, F *et al.,* 2021). In this section, multiple threat detection approaches are detailed in elaborated manner.

Behavioral Modelling Intrusion Detection System (BMIDS) is proposed by utilizing immunity-inspired algorithms for categorizing behavioral patterns (Ahmed, M & Pathan, ASK 2020). This anomaly detection system is based on IoT behaviors. For designing appropriate behaviour models activities are monitored making use of smart simulation environment. Objective of BMIDS is to maximize detection sensitivity through IoT end devices for diagnosing uniqueness amid behavioral patterns.

Semi-supervised anomaly detection system making use of k-means algorithm is proposed for detecting network attacks (http://www.trend micro .com). Cluster is formed with the help of k means algorithm by classifying typical samples in training phase. Distance based threshold value is computed to differentiate normal and abnormal samples by utilizing validation dataset. Samples which are far away from the centres of cluster are considered as anomalies. Labelled dataset NSL-KDD is utilized for testing proposed system's performance and detection result is attained with 80.119% accuracy.

With the integration of SDN and blockchain, IoT based distributed Software Defined Networking (SDN) architecture is implemented (Stone, J 2019). Interaction among nodes is permitted without the help of central controller. Entire IoT controller environment is connected for effective communication by implementing distributed block chain. Amalgamation of flow control analyzer and packet migration components supports network functioning during attacking scenario. For accurate attack detection, various IoT device oriented attack simulations like ARP poisoning, DDoS and fake topology attacks are designed. Proposed technique reduces attack window detection time and it also fastens attack mitigation.

On the basis of sampling with Least Square Support Vector Machine (LS-SVM) intrusions are detected (Lei, X *et al.,* 2018). This method has two stages. Training and testing datasets are combined for determining the size of sample. Optimum Allocation (OA) scheme is used defining the size of training and testing. At first stage dataset is categorized into predetermined subgroups of arbitrary instances. In the second stage LS-SVM is incorporated for intrusion detection by extracting the samples which uses selective instances as input. Proposed algorithm is referred as Optimum Allocation-based Least Square Support Vector Machine (OA-LS-SVM) algorithm. Further KDD 99 database is used for system's performance evaluation.

Network behaviors of IoT end devices are extracted and statistical analysis method is utilized for Doshi *et al.,'s* anomaly detection method (Rodrigues, B 2015). It is found that Mirai and BASHLITE are two highly infectious botnets which compromised most of the IoT end devices. Mirroring port of switch is used for capturing typical network flow and 115 features are extracted. For maintaining separate model for every IoT end device neural network auto encoder is used. With the sum of mean and standard deviation of samples, anomaly threshold value is computed. On the basis of experimental results, 100% True Positive Rate (TPR) is attained with some alarm elevations.

Mehmood *et al.,* proposed NB-MAIDS which concentrates on the improvisation of intrusion detection accuracy by utilizing network behaviors of IoT for feature selection (Fernandes, E *et al.,* 2017). Detecting and preventing DDoS attack traffic of the devices associated with the home network is considered as ultimate aim. Naive Bayes classification algorithm plays vital role for Intrusion Detection Systems which is a light weighted algorithm used for pattern matching. Better performance is obtained while implementing NB algorithm with multiple agents. Secured IoT network layer is aimed from malicious DDoS traffic. Based on the experiment results detection accuracy is achieved as 91-99%.

Ahmed & Rajput worked in order to safeguard IoT end devices against DDoS attacks (Stoffer, V 2013). Development of IDSs is done using Naïve Bayes classification algorithm. Multi agent system comprised with a collection of autonomous agents is incorporated for learning IoT end devices. Then, Multi agent IDSs are deployed for observing abnormal network traffic amid nodes during communication. There are four various agents utilized which are collector agent, system monitoring agent, actuator agent and communication agent with respective roles. Data collection is performed by collector agent and the entire multi agent system is monitored by system monitoring agent. Actuator agent is meant for reacting against the detected attackers. At last communication agent communicates with other agents of the network regarding detection results. Results show that attack detection and prevention is fast and entire load is dispersed for agents in appropriate manner.

Block chain based intra and inter-domain DDoS attacks mitigation method is proposed (Kayastha, N *et al.,* 2014). It permits various SDN based domains for transferring secured information regarding attacks without any centralization method. Thus it provides attack mitigation in effective manner against attacks. Further cost reduction of useless attack traffic is done. Smart contract-based method is proposed making use of Ethereum smart contract technology to enhance security. In addition, flow sampling method is utilized for measuring randomness of data. At last, automatic detection of inside domain's traffic anomalies is succeeded using Bayes-based scheme. Results depicts effective solution in terms of cost and flexible anomaly flow detection.

Anomaly detection framework is developed by adopting SDN, ML and fog computing technology (Spreitzer *et al.,* 2018). It affords network control in the infrastructures of cloud and network edge. Various features are selected for ML computation and comparative parameters are formulated on the basis of cloud and fog network of IoT. For increasing DDoS attack detection accuracy, Recurrent Neural Network (RNN), Multi-Layer Perceptron (MLP) and Alternate Decision Tree (ADT) are utilized. An access list with a set of blacklist prefixes is maintained by every controller in during mitigation stage. It is concluded that comparing with cloud infrastructure, fog computing performs better while detecting attacks.

A collaborative and intelligent network-based IDS, Search is proposed by Nguyen *et al.,* for software defined cloud IoT infrastructure (https://www.cloudflare.com). Detection of anomalies and SDN based IoT gateway devices policy formulation are combined making use of hierarchical layered intelligent IDS nodes for braking malicious traffic quickly. Collaborative attack detection is performed by locating multiple IDS at network edge and cloud. ML classification algorithms like Support Vector Machine (SVM) and Self Organize Map (SOM) are utilized for detecting anomalies and making policies at every network level. Data samples of 30K from 3 various datasets are extracted along with TCP and ICMP features. It provides better accuracy for anomaly detection than existing centralized methods while evaluating performance.

Table 3.1 Summary of Existing Works

Research Work	Features	Technology used	Algorithms of classification	Detection method
Sharma *et al.,* (2017)	All traffic, scanning attacks	Block chain, SDN	Mean and standard deviation technique	Traffic statistic
Doshi *et al.,* (2018)	Behaviour learning, packet header fields, aggregate flow	Traditional Internet	Machine Learning	Anomaly detection
Mehmood *et al* (2018)	Multi agent, DDoS traffic	Traditional Internet	Naïve Bayes algorithm	NB-MAIDS
Houda *et*	Anomaly	Block chain,	Collaborative	Bayes-base

al., (2019)	detection, Inter and intra-domain collaborative DDoS mitigation	SDN	approach, smart contract-based approach, flow sampling method	scheme
Shafi *et al.*, (2019)	Cloud infrastructure, DDoS attacks	SDN and Fog computing	Entropy based	Anomaly detector
Nguyen *et al.*, (2019)	Reconnaissance Attacks	Block chain, SDN, Fog computing	Machine learning	Multiple IDS
Rathore *et al.*, (2019)	Host-based, time-based, content and basic features	Block chain, SDN, Fog computing, Edge computing	Deep learning algorithms	Dynamic update of attack detection model
Yang *et al.*, (2019)	DDoS attacks, IoT gateway as IDS	SDN and Edge computing	Machine learning	Multiple point defence mechanism
Wazid *et al.*, (2019)	Remaining energy amount of an IoT sensor, Routing attacks	Edge computing	2 stages approach	RAD-EI
Singh *et al.*, (2020)	MEC environment, Three classifiers	Mobile edge computing	C4.5 classifier, Naïve Bayes, Meta adaboost M1,	Hybrid Intrsion detection

Another decentralized IoT network security architecture Block SecIoTNet is developed on the basis of block chain (cdn.iotwf.com). For effective attack detection SDN, block chain and fog computing technologies are used. To monitor and examine the entire IoT network continuously, SDN is used. Similarly, Ethereum block chain technology is used for attack detection in decentralized manner which mitigates the issues related to single point of failure problem. Attack at fog node and edge node are detected are simplified with the help of fog and edge computing. Earlier attack detection and mitigation is possible with low memory limitations, inexpensive computation and minimum latency. Edge network's attack detection and mitigation is implemented using deep learning algorithms. Attack detection model dynamically updated to increase detection efficiency. Anomaly classifier is associated with different data formats like numeric, binary and nominal. It is observed that proposed framework mitigate IoT attacks with minimum time.

Yang *et al.,* concentrated on detecting and mitigating IoT based DDoS attacks making use of SDN (Farahani, S 2008). Précised features of IoT traffic are considered while edge computing technology is applied. Distributed anomaly detection method is faster and it didn't affect centralized controller during the scenarios of IoT attacks. Edge gateway process the detection request which avoids controller intervention even in real time environment. Flow level features are taken as input for feature extraction. Mininetis used for experiment's simulation purpose. To categorize genuine flows amid DDoS flows three various ML algorithms are utilized. Among them RF provided better results with 100% True Positive.

RAD-EI is an intrusion detection scheme proposed by Wazid *et al.,* which is focused on IoT routing attacks (Morgner, P *et al.,* 2016). Typical traffic flow can be deviated and interrupt by malicious IoT sensors in routing attack. Every malicious sensor forward packets towards its nearer attacker node. Here anticipated information will not be received to edge node. This detection scheme has two phases. During phase 1, doubted attack nodes list is captured while they are available in network. Doubted attacker is discovered based on the computed energy level (drained battery). In phase 2, IoT sensor is decided whether it is attacker or normal node. Any IoT device which doesn't receive any reply messages then it is considered as attacker node.

Mobile edge computing based hybrid intrusion detection framework is proposed. It is focused on unknown attacks which is based on ML. Traffic of MEC environment is analyzed for identifying intrusions. Three distinct classifiers are utilized in this framework which are C4.5 classifier, Naïve Bayes classifier and Meta Adaboost M1. Based on the experimental results it is observed that proposed framework has 90.25% accuracy with 1.1% FAR. Security of proposed framework is analyzed using game theoretical model. While comparing to existing models it provides better results.

3.1.3 IoT and Edge Computing Background

A. IoT basic Components and Architecture

IoT environment is a universal distributed network which allows communication among various devices/computers. Communication is carried either as in wired or wireless manner. Data exchange is ensured using such communication channel. Multiple physical objects, sensors are connected and it is applicable in various application areas which is effective in terms of cost and technology. IoT economy is vast worldwide. For effective IoT environment multiple IoT components are interconnected to build basement for IoT architecture. IoT devices, IoT connectivity, IoT platforms and IoT Apps/Interfaces are the four basic components of IoT ecosystem. Those are layered for providing different IoT solutions based on their convenient and requirement.

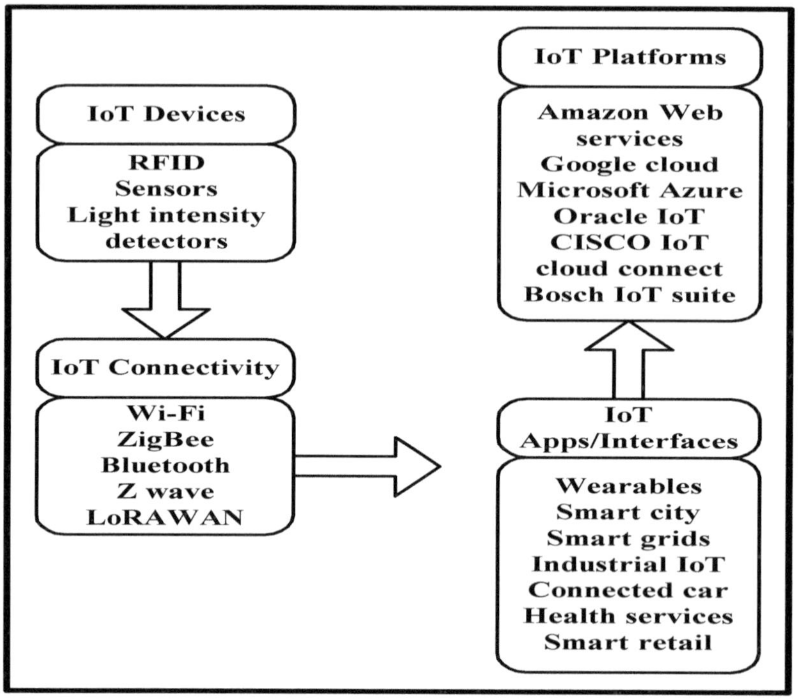

Figure 3.1 Basic IoT Components

Due to the dynamical nature of IoT domain day by day, novel technologies are applied and adopted. It is difficult to implement one architecture as main reference for all solutions (Angrishi, K 2017). Different research works are carried for developing IoT architectures in effective manner. Figure 3.1 depicts the four basic components of IoT ecosystem.

IoT devices component contains the physical hardware devices and sensors. Based on the IoT solution various hardware devices are utilized. Data is interchanged by the device in centralized manner. To resolve the connectivity issues of hardware devices, IoT gateways are used amid physical environment and IoT platform. Thus, IoT devices make their connection and data exchange is carried within the domain.

Various IoT architectures are proposed considering all the basic components. Among them three layer, four layer and five layer IoT architectures are usual and frequently used. In three layer IoT architecture, there are three basic blocks which are perception layer, network layer and application layer (Langner, R 2011)-(Petrov, C 2019). Perception layer deals with devices and sensors. Network layer acts as an interface between perception and application layer where, application layer states every IoT based applications.

Shortcomings of three layer IoT architecture are overcome by four layer IoT architecture in which fourth additional layer namely support layer is added (Azmoodeh, A *et al.*, 2018). Support layer is mainly meant for security. Two main tasks of support layer are authentication and forwarding information towards network layer. Five layer IoT architecture mainly concentrated over the constraints of security as well as memory (Sakhnini, J *et al.*, 2019). Additional two layers are business and processing.

B. Edge Computing

Market of edge computing is forecasted with the increase of USD 87.3 billion to USD 36.5 billion in between the years 2021 to 2026 (https://www.sonicwall.com). Pandemic period of COVID 19 increased the global adoption of technology for the large scale sized organizations as well as SME because of its cost effective. With enhanced data control, minimal costs and faster processing edge computing fetches computation and data storage under same roof once data is generated. It is expected that in the year 2025, 75% of enterprises will process data using edge computing. In real time data processing, reduced data throughput and secured data are the major advantages of edge computing. Latency problems related with cloud methods are avoided. Local data processing is performed at edge gateways which ensures data evaluation. Cloud dependency is reduced with this decentralized data processing.

Edge computing is applicable in various areas such as automated vehicles, healthcare systems, security solutions, retail advertising, smart speakers and video conferences. Figure 3.2 depicts the basic edge computing based IoT architecture. Today edge computing has become as enhancement of cloud by incorporating various functions like data aggregation, local data storage, Monitoring based on AI and Machine to Machine (M2M) communication. While applying edge computing to IoT environment it is contained with three elements namely edge, edge device and edge gateway.

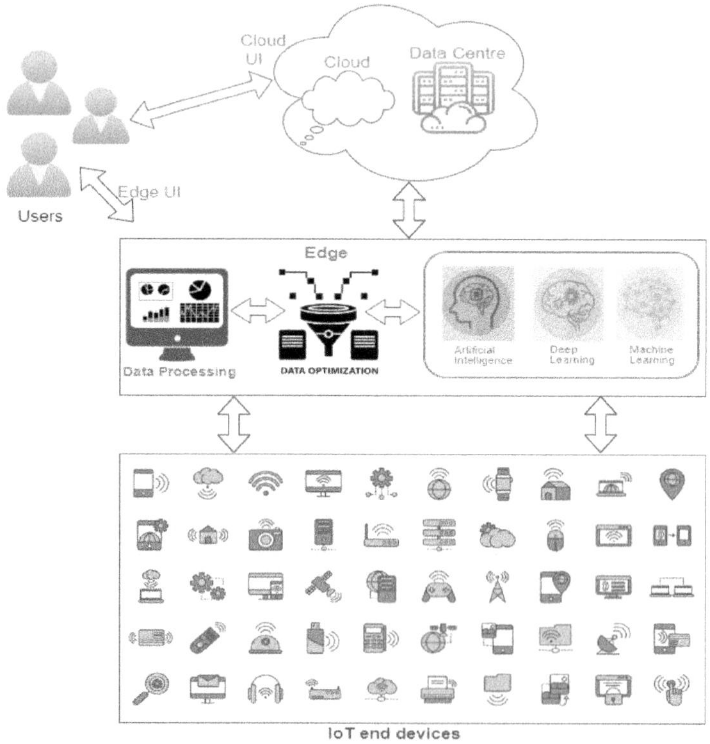

Figure 3.2 Edge Computing based IoT Architecture

3.1.4 Proposed Framework – Edge AI Computing

Proposed security framework is divided into four phases which are feature extraction, edge computing, training & testing and validation. Proposed framework is portrayed in Figure 3.3.

A. Feature Extraction

Key processes of this first phase are data collection and data preprocessing. Input of this phase is dataset and output obtained is feature set. Network intrusion dataset UNSW-NB15 is utilized which is comprised with nine various recent attacks such as analyzis, exploits, worms, backdoors, Denial of Service (DoS), shell code, reconnaissance, generic and fuzzers (https://www.f5.com). This dataset contains 49 features and it is divided into five main categories based on flow, content, basic, time and additional. The main features of the dataset are IP address, port number, attributes of TCP/IP and HTTP, network's time attributes, general purpose and connection features. UNSW-NB15 dataset overcomes the drawbacks of KDDCUP 99 and NSLKDD datasets and it seems better than them while considering number of attacks which is four types (DoS, PRB, U2R, R2L) only.

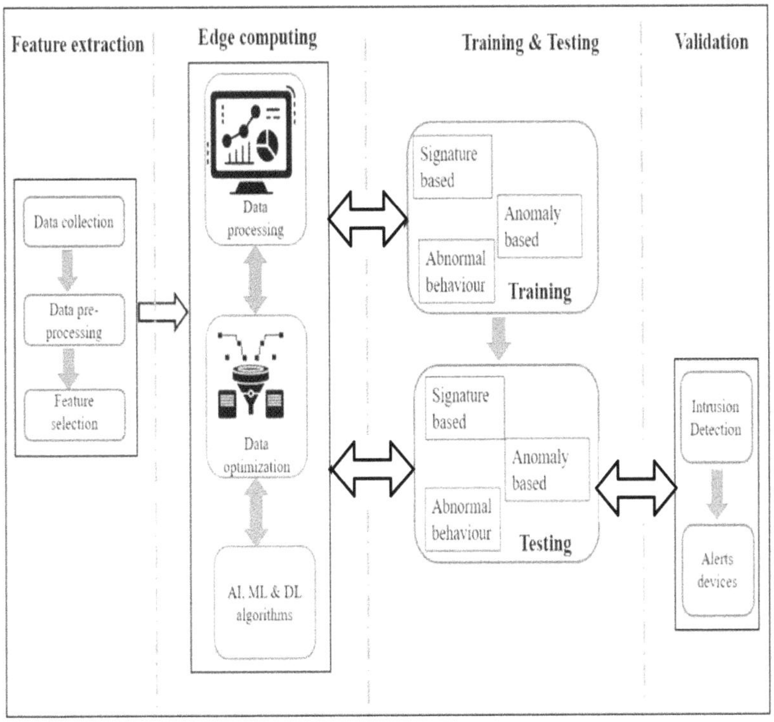

Figure 3.3 Proposed Framework

During data pre-processing, size of UNSW-NB15 dataset is minimized by removing the repeated data. Clustering method is helpful for discovering the similarities of behavior among various types of dataset. Foremost, labels of dataset are eliminated. Cluster's quality and its required count is obtained by applying Silhouette coefficient and k-mean cluster algorithm is incorporated to manage cluster configurations. Testing is performed making use of random data. In feature selection process, features of dataset are chosen by computing the value of Information Gain (IG). IG value defines the significance of feature from the collected dataset. If the value is high, then it is considered that significance of that feature also high among others. IG is computed as follows:

$$IG(S, A) = H(S) - H(S|A)$$

where IG(S, A) refers dataset information and S refers to the random variable, H(S) defines the dataset entropy (purity of dataset) before the occurrences of some change and H(S|A) states dataset's conditional entropy while taking input variable A. Conditional entropy is computed by dividing dataset into clusters in every value observed.

$$H(S|A) = \text{sum v in a } SA(v)/S * H(SA(v))$$

Where SA(v)/S defines the ratio of examples count of dataset with variable A which is valued v. H(SA(v)) defines entopy of sample cluster with variable A which is valued v. Based on the IG value, feature set is defined and forwarded for further phases.

B. Edge Computing

In this proposed framework edge computing phase is divided into three parts which are data processing, data optimization and AI, ML and DL based algorithms selection. Feature set is considered as input for this phase. Further, data is optimized in this phase for improving better accuracy in intrusion detection. In this phase, data breach related attacks are avoided by choosing appropriate algorithms related to AI, ML and DL. Figure 3.4 shows the experimental setup used in this research.

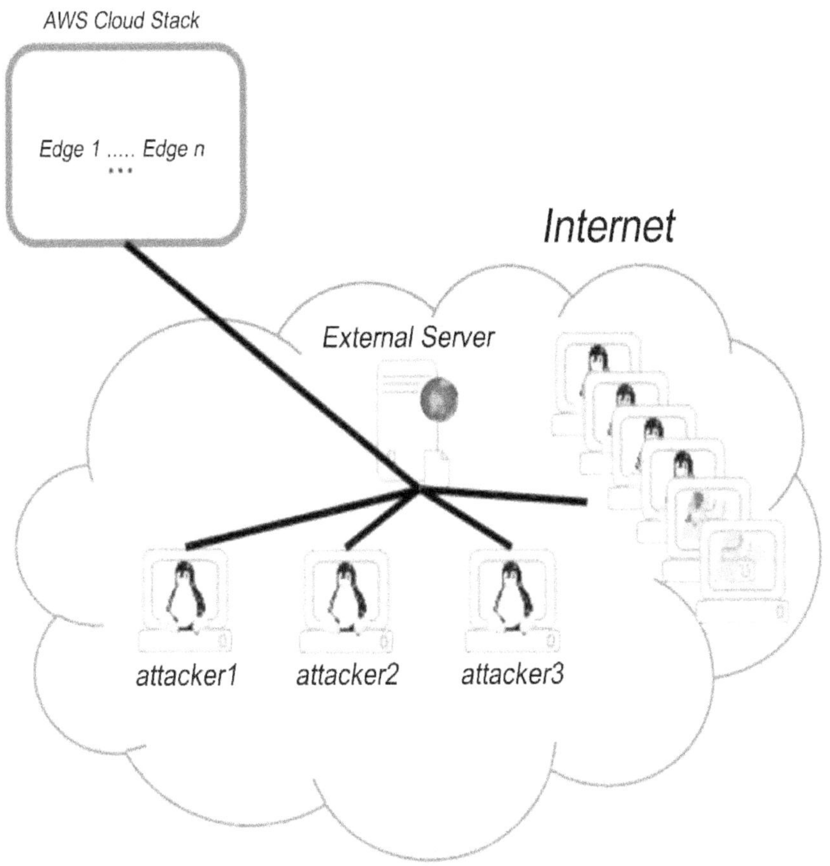

Figure 3.4 Experimental Setup

3.2 AN AUTOMATED SECURITY MODEL FOR DATA DRIVEN IoT ECOSYSTEM

3.2.1 Introduction

IoT market value is anticipated as $1102.6 billion in 2026 which is nearly 6 times larger than the value of 2018 with 24.7% Compound Annual Growth Rate (CAGR) during the projection time. Most of the market share holders belonged to banking and financial services after IT related services. In addition its market space is extended with high percentage towards healthcare and government related applications. The massive development of IoT presents the ability for billions of devices to connect and share data for several applications. Further its enormous amount of growth created various issues regarding security and privacy of IoT ecosystem which is considered as primary concern to be resolved. Based on recent research report, market worth of universal IoT security is predicted as $40.3 billion in the year 2026 (Sfar *et al.,* 2018, Sood, K *et al.,* 2020, Al-Garadi, MA *et al.,* 2020, Granjal, J *et al.,* 2015, Meidan, Y *et al.,* 2017). In 2021 it was $14.9 billion and 22.1% CAGR is observed for this prediction duration. Microsoft, AWS, Google, IBM, Cisco, Ericson and Thales are considered as primary players in IoT security market. Network security part of IoT applications is target with various threats and exploitations and it has highest market value (https://www.trgdatacenters.com).

Various security vulnerability cases of IoT ecosystem and its devices are reported because of mass volume and inadequate security sources turned the interests of attackers for impairing the system. As all the devices of IoT network are interconnected together domain name, providers are targeted by applying Denial of Service (DoS) attack towards various famous websites like Twitter, GitHub and others (Sood, K *et al.,* 2020). In Nov 2021, more than million devices and routers are targeted by Botenago malware with 30 plus various exploitations and AT &T Alien labs discovered it (Al-Garadi, MA *et al.,* 2020). Botenagois based on Google's open source programming language Golang. It generates one backdoor and utilizes port number 19412 for targeting attacks.

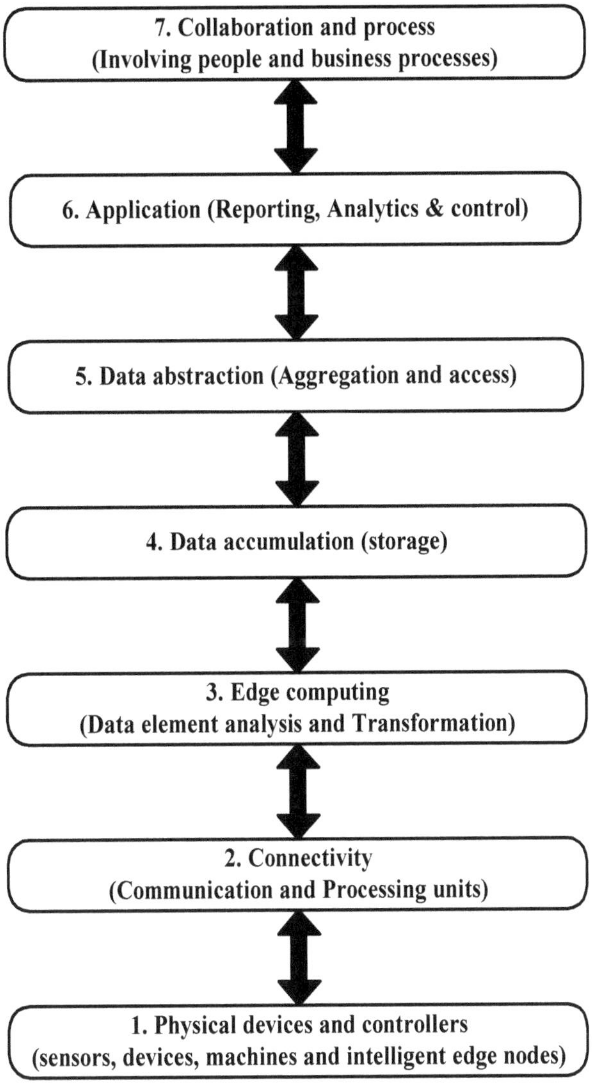

Figure 3.5 IoT Reference Model

Mirai botnet is another dangerous ones which targeted various connected devices making use of constant usernames and passwords (Granjal, J *et al.,* 2015). Internet Connected Autonomous Vehicles (CAVs) are also targeted by taking control of them. Smart IoT devices are light weighted for executing applications in embedded CPUs with minimum capacity of memory, battery and such computational limitations are converted as attack vectors of system's security and privacy. In the year 2014, seven layered IoT reference model is launched at IoT world forum by Intel, IBM and Cisco in order to educate developers and research fellows of IT departments and hasten the adopting technologies of IoT (Meidan, Y *et al.,* 2017). Figure 3.5 depicts the IoT reference model.

IoT devices share sensitive information via core controllers. Stuxnet malware targets précised control system of industries (Uranium Enrichment Plant) which postponed the development of Iran's nuclear weapons program (Iqbal, H *et al.,* 2020). IoT Technologies are applied in various real time applications for effective and efficient enhancement like smart cities, smart homes, surveillance and healthcare. Authentication mechanisms of devices as well as the IoT ecosystem should be implemented strongly for avoiding any negotiation.

The key contribution of the work are summarized as below:

- AI is applied for detecting malwares from benign files in the IoT ecosystem.
- Deep learning based model is proposed by applying the advancements towards security after Machine learning.
- To ensure effective communication without intervention of any malicious attacker, neural network auto encoders are utilized.

3.2.2 Related Work

Several research works are done for securing IoT devices and ecosystem (George, G & Thampi, SM 2018). Deep learning algorithms and IoT standard datasets are reviewed in detail to enhance the security requirements by considering various security concerns of IoT environment (Jeon, J *et al.,* 2020). Cyber-attack detection method is implemented based on analyzing the IoT security and its importance through software defined security (Ullah & Mahmoud, QH 2021). Recent research works are detailed in this section and summary is provided in Table 3.2.

Malicious attack detection framework is proposed for IoT networks by employing four DL models namely Multi-Layer Perceptron (MLP), DNNs, CNNs and auto encoder (Sudhakaran & Pradeep 2021). Keras deep learning library is used for detecting malicious activities. Two different dataset are utilized which are UNSW-NB15 (Al-Garadi, MA *et al.,* 2020) and NSL-KDD99. As per the experimental results, proposed frame work gained 99.28% accuracy and 95.76% accuracy for the respective DS1 and DS2. In addition RMSE and F1 score metrics are also used for performance evaluation. Multimodal Deep Learning model is studied applied for detecting android malwares making use of various types of features which are related to the properties of android apps (https://www.marketsandmarkets.com). Feature vector generation methods are suggested for malware property representation by considering features like string, method opcode, method API, shared library function opcode, permission, component and environment. DNN is used for classification purpose. Performance evaluation is done with the set of 41,260 samples. Simulator datasets are used for this framework and 98% accuracy attained.

To improve detection performance in IoT environment Deep Reinforcement Learning (DRL) is applied and DQN is developed as a watermark model for security enhancement (https://cybersecurity.att.com). Virtual IP circuit's distance vectors are trained using ANN. Every Look Up Table's (LUT) virtual position characteristics are used for computing mapping relationship. Neural network based fault tolerance, watermark detection, real- time detection and self-learning increase performance. While considering the results, 70% accuracy only attained making use of XC2V500

FPGA dataset which is considered as lesser. IoT botnet detection system is developed with the analysis of DNS services in IoT based smart city applications. It is a 2 level framework in which DNS logs are investigated for DL based Domain Generation Algorithm (DGA) domain name. Self-learning methods are applied for detecting bots and APTs. Familiar DNS features like length, entropy and n-gram are visualized as histogram, scatter plot and density plot. DL based Long Short Term Memory (LSTM) and Recurrent Neural Network (RNN) model are further used. Its accuracy is evaluated by comparing with standard models like SVM, KNN and LR. RNN of this model contains strong class of DNN which is used for distributing data in sequenced manner. Results depict that 92% accuracy is obtained and Bot-IoT dataset is utilized.

Supervised learning algorithm, K-Nearest Neighbor (KNN) is utilized for intrusion detection and mitigation in IoT environment (https://www.globalsign.com). KNN connects fresh data points with existing related points via given data by filtration. Fresh data is matched with K - nearest neighbors and then making use of that parameters model is involved for training and clustering. KNN works as simple by classifying sensor nodes with minimum two parameters which are K value and distance function like Euclidean. Its performance is poor while performing with huge datasets and networks. Noisy data needs more cost for finding distance in between objects. In addition KNN is not suitable for high dimensional data which may increase complexity due to outsized parameters.

Small sample DDoS attacks detection method is designed making use of deep transfer learning (Melamed, T 2018). Transfer performance index is first designed and then transfer performance values of various networks of source domain are compared. As transfer performance value of 8LANN is elevated with 10 to 20% while comparing other networks. 8LANN networks are involved for training small samples source domain SYN-Type DDoS attacks detection and result is obtained as 99.08% accuracy.

Three preprocessing methods namely direct, weighted and compressed are proposed for CNN based IDSs making use of least information of communication protocol, size and offset for conquering challenges of DL based IDS (Ahmed, M & Pathan, ASK 2020). Direct method uses the properties of kernel, where weighted and compressed methods utilize network information. Here, CNN is utilized for detecting outliers and malwares and it performs better. KDD Cup 99, NSL- KDD and DARPA datasets are utilized for training and testing phases. 88% accuracy is achieved on the basis of experimentation results. Brute-Force Attack Method (BFAM) is applied to detect the GAN related attacks making use of the datasets such as ADFA- LD, DREBIN and NSL-KDD for validation purpose (http://www.trend micro .com). Based on the results, 91% accuracy is attained.

DL based Deep Belief Network (DBN) model is proposed for detecting intrusion in Internet of Medical Things (IoMT) environment (Stone, J 2019). CICIDS 2017 dataset is used for analyzing the performance of the model in order to detect attacks and anomalies. Accuracy, recall, precision, F1-score and detection rate are the performance metrics considered for results evaluation. Based on the results, DBN model attained accuracy of 99.37%, 97.93%, 97.71%, 96.67%, 96.37%, 97.71% and 98.37% for the respective classes of normal, Botnet, Brute Force , DoS/DDoS, Infiltration, Ports and Web attack. To detect DDoS attacks in IoT environment IDS is proposed where DL technique is hybridized with multi object optimization method (Lei, X *et al.,* 2018). IDS is developed by combining techniques of Jumping Gene adapted NSGA-II multi-objective optimization method for data dimension reduction and CNN incorporated LSTM for attack classification. IDS is validated making use of CISIDS 2017 datasets in High Performance

Computers (HPCs) and it attained 99.03% accuracy and 99.36% F1 - score with fivefold reduction training time. In addition obtained results are compared with other state of the art and ML algorithms.

Deep Transfer Learning (DTL) method is applied for attack detection in IoT networks (Rodrigues, B 2015). DTL permits learning from the collected unlabeled data of various IoT devices. This model is developed on the basis of two auto encoders. Training of first auto encoder is done over source domain datasets in supervised manner and on other side training of second auto encoder is done over target domains datasets in unsupervised manner. Bottleneck layers of both auto encoders are represented. Then second auto encoder is utilized for attack detection from input samples of target domain. Performance evaluation is done by using recent IoT dataset and 94% accuracy is achieved.

DL based phishing detection system is implemented. CNN is applied on URLs for phishing web pages detection (Fernandes, E *et al.,* 2017). On the basis of experimentation results, it is observed that implemented system attained 98% accuracy which is better performance than previous model. There is no feature engineering done and URL based automatic feature extraction is performed via the hidden layers of CNN.

Table 3.2 Summary of Recent Works

Research	Features	Proposed Model/Algorithm	Performance results
Nagisetty *etal.,*(2019)	Keras deep learning library, Malicious attack, UNSW-NB15,NSL- KDD99 datasets	Multi LayerPerceptron, DNNs, CNNs, autoencoder	99.28% accuracy for DS1 , 95.76% accuracy for DS2
Kim *et al.,*(2019)	Malware attacks, Simulator dataset	DNN or RNN	98% accuracy

Liang *et al.*,(2020)	Watermark detection,Real- Time detection, XC2V500 FPGA dataset	DRL(Deep Reinforcement Learning),DQN	70% accuracy
Vinayakumar R *et al.*,(2020)	Botnet detection, Bot-IoT dataset	C-CMU	0.92% accuracy
Ravi *et al.*,(2020)	Data Deluge, intrusion detection, NSL-KDD dataset	SSML DFNN-RRS- K means (SDRK), SSML Semi Supervised ML	99.78% accuracy
He *et al.*, (2020)	SYN-Type DDoS attacks detection, Simulator dataset	8LANN	99.08 accuracy
Jo *et al.*, (2020)	Outlier detection, Malware detection, KDD Cup 99,NSL-KDD,DARPA datasets	CNN	88% accuracy
Zhang *et al.*, (2020)	GAN-based attack detection, ADFA-LD,DREBIN,NSL-KDD datasets	BFAM (Brute-Force Attack Method)	91% accuracy
Manimurugan *et al.*, (2020)	Anomaly detection, CICIDS 2017 dataset	DBN(Deep Belief Network)	normal class-99.37%,Botnet class-97.93%,Brute Force class-96.67%,DoS,DDos-96.37%,Infiltration- 97.71%,Web Attack- 98.37%

Patidar *et al.*, (2020)	Rmove attack by software installation, CICIDS 2017 dataset	Multi-headed CNN	99.38% accuracy
Roopak *et al.*, (2020)	DDoS attack detection, CICIDS 2017 dataset	CNN+LSTM	99.03% accuracy
Vu *et al.*, (2020)	Cyber-attack detection, MMD-AE dataset	DTL (Deep Transfer Learning)	0.94% accuracy
Singh *et al.*, (2020)	Phishing Detection, Isbi 2017 dataset	CNN	98% accuracy
Jiang *et al.*, (2020)	Multi-channel attack detection, KDD Cup 1999,NSL- KDD datasets	Voting algorithm	98.64% accuracy
Kewei *et al.*, (2021)	Fraud detection, IEEE-CIS dataset	SVM +NB	0.958 accuracy

Multi-channel intelligent attack detection method is proposed on the basis of LSTM-RNNs (Stoffer, V 2013). To decide whether traffic is under attack, voting algorithm is proposed for attaining more accuracy. It is scalable and neural network is chosen based on data features. Data preprocessing, feature abstraction, and multi-channel training and detection phases are integrated for enhanced detection. Classifiers are developed by multi-channel processing by training with various feature types. KDD Cup 1999 and NSL-KDD datasets are used for evaluation and it achieved 98.64% accuracy. DL based neural network algorithm is proposed for detecting credit card frauds (Kayastha, N *et al.,* 2014). Various methods are employed which contains feature engineering, memory compression, mixed precision and ensemble loss for improving performance. For evaluating this model IEEE-CIS fraud dataset is utilized which is contained with 1 million records. Results depict with the attainment of 95.8% accuracy.

3.2.3 Preliminaries

A. IoT Layered Architecture

The basic components of IoT architecture are applications, Intelligent IoT (IIoT) devices and Gateways, networks and datacenters. Applications permit end users for connecting with IoT ecosystem and manipulating physical world. Gateways, networks connect IoT devices with internet world and datacenters are useful for affording data storage and analytics. Intelligent IoT devices are equipped in various application areas. In addition multi-layered architecture can be enlarged based on these fundamental components. Intelligent IoT devices are hosted in perception layer. Connectivity layer transfers data amid physical world and cloud through networks and gateways. Processing layer performs data accumulation and management using datacenters. Application layer resolves the problems of analytics, reporting and device control related to users. Edge computing layer, business layer and security layer are further layers. Edge computing layer performs data processing. Data based business decisions are taken in business layer. All the layers are included by security layer. IoT layered architecture is portrayed in Figure 3.6.

B. Deep Learning Model

Deep learning is the subset of machine learning in which Artificial Intelligence techniques are utilized. Learning process is implemented with the help of samples. Multiple layers are developed hierarchically once appropriate feature set is obtained from feature extraction. DL is applied in various applications such as automation, image processing and natural language processing. In general, DL models are developed on the basis of either supervised or unsupervised learning where, training approaches may differ with respect to the requirements of model. Input data of supervised learning models are label based. Unsupervised models are other side which are based on unlabeled data. Deep Neural Network (DNN), Convolutional Neural Network (CNN), Recurrent Neural Network (RNN), Long Short Term Memory Networks (LSTMs), Generative Adversarial Networks (GANs), Multi-Layer Perceptron's (MLPs), Radial Basis Function Networks (RBFNs), Self-Organizing Maps (SOMs), Restricted Boltzmann Machines(RBMs), Deep Belief Networks (DBNs) and auto encoders are the standard models (Spreitzer, R *et al.,* 2018, https://www.cloudflare.com, cdn.iotwf.com, Farahani, S 2008, Morgner, P *et al.,* 2016, Simplício, MA *et al.,* Angrishi, K 2017).

Artificial Intelligence includes its own extraction in the methodologies of deep learning and it is represented in the form of Neural Network and most of the operations are carried using Graphical Processing Units (GPUs). End to end learning is attained by the own algorithms of DL and real time data provided. In general, DL is provided with the sequence of layers.

C. Datasets Utilized

UNSW-NB15 and Bot-IoT datasets are employed in both training and testing phases. UNSW-NB15 is a network intrusion based dataset which includes 2,57,673 data records (Langner, R 2011, Petrov, C 2019, Azmoodeh, A *et al.,* 2018). It is deal with nine distinct attacks containing DDoS, DoS, backdoors, worms and fuzzers.

Bot-IoT dataset is associated with real time network environment (Sakhnini, J *et al.,* 2019, https://www.sonicwall.com, Jurn J *et al.,* year). It has 7,20,00,000 records and its size is 69.3 GB size of captured pcap files. It is also downloadable in csv format with size of 16.7 GB. BoT-IoT dataset is comprised with various attacks namely DoS, DDoS, OS and service scan, key logging attack and data exfiltration attack (https://www.f5.com).

3.2.4 Proposed Deep Learning Model

Most the IoT attacks are happening at the stages of data collection and data processing. To avoid attacking scenarios on those stages they should be monitored carefully to detect attacks and abnormal activities should be reported earlier. In general, input data of every entity in IoT ecosystem is analyzed on the basis of usual interaction behavior. If abnormal or malicious activities found, they should be reported for avoiding attacks. After utilization of ML methods, DL methods are incorporated for sound data investigation. DL methods are currently utilized intelligent attack detection and anonymous attacks are also detected by learning from the previous attack incidents. Proposed DL model is presented in Figure 3.7.

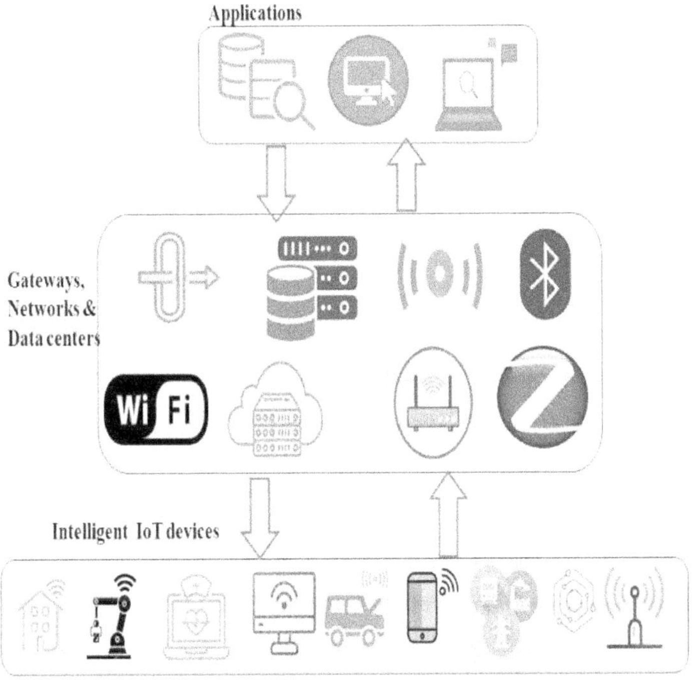

Figure 3.6 IoT Layered Architecture

A. Data Collection and Accumula1tion

As IoT ecosystem (Figure 3.6) has global standard for effective communication within the network, data sharing should be performed in secured manner to avoid data breaches. Data collection is first stage, which is done based on the requirements. Various datasets are used for data collection and in some cases real time dynamic data is utilized. Data collection is performed in application layer of the IoT layered architecture. In IoT ecosystem each and every connected device is sharing millions of data within the system. Each data has distinct format, size and speed. Appropriate data segregation from bulk streams is a crucial concern which should be resolved at the earliest. Intelligence factors collection is necessary for understanding such unstructured data of photos and videos. It is essential to understand data requirements as effectively. In IoT layered structure perception layer involves in data accumulation.

B. Data Preprocessing

Data preprocessing phase of this proposed system is comprised with sub phases such as data cleaning, data visualization and data sampling in order to enhance feature selection in optimized manner. Data cleaning involves in the removal of unappropriate data from the datasets to obtain data in appropriate format. As unlabeled dynamic data is used for processing data cleaning process is required. After cleaning it is implemented with data visualization process which is useful for understanding outliers and patterns of the dataset for avoiding malformed data. Histograms and scatterplots are used as the tools for data visualization.

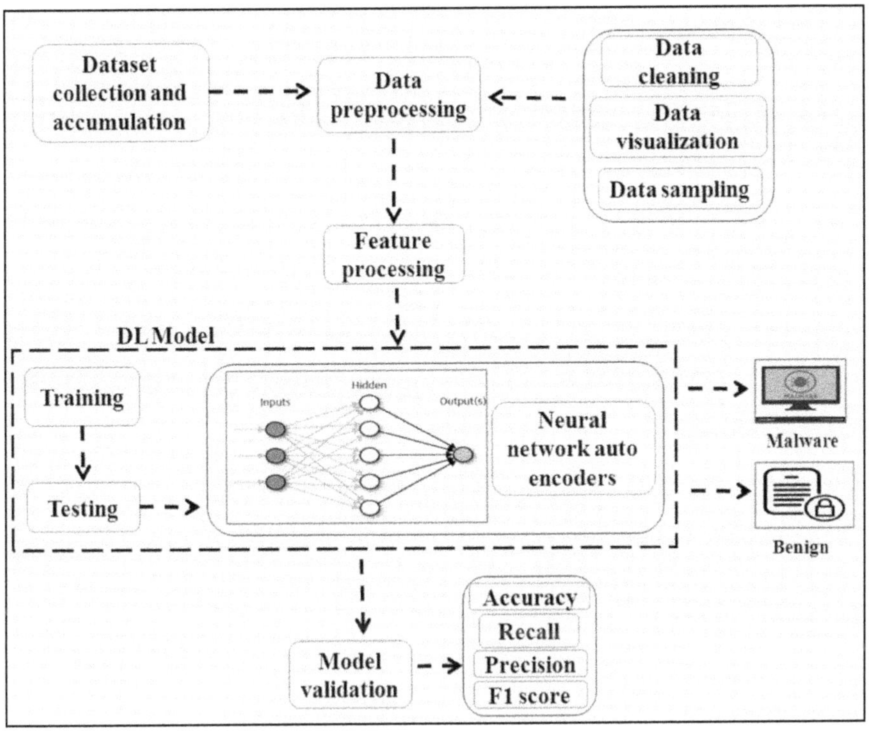

Figure 3.7 Proposed DL Model

As IoT data volume is vast and its time series is also not regular among devices in the network. Linear resampling method is incorporated for making IoT data in consistent and regular manner. It is involved with two stages. In the first stage, raw data is unstamped making use of mean aggregation function and linear interpolation. In second stage, data is down sampled with the help of straight forward fill aggregation.

C. Feature Preprocessing

For training phase more than 70% data records are used and for testing phase remaining 30% data records are used by considering a variety of attack and regular from both UNSW-NB15 and Bot-IoT datasets. Feature vector is created after obtaining cleaned data from the previous stage. Feature optimization is applied for selecting appropriate feature from the utilized datasets.

D. Deep Learning Model

DL model is comprised with training and testing stages where two distinct datasets UNSW-NB15 and Bot-IoT are utilized for enhanced evaluation and results. Neural network auto encoders are also utilized for effective attack prediction. As the proposed model follows unsupervised learning and utilizes unlabeled data as input, Artificial Neural Network (ANN) autoencoderis used for effective performance. Noise data (irrelevant data) are removed by applying dimensionality reduction during training process and from that autoencoder learns to encode or represent data. Figure 3.8 depicts the architecture of Convolutional Neural Network.

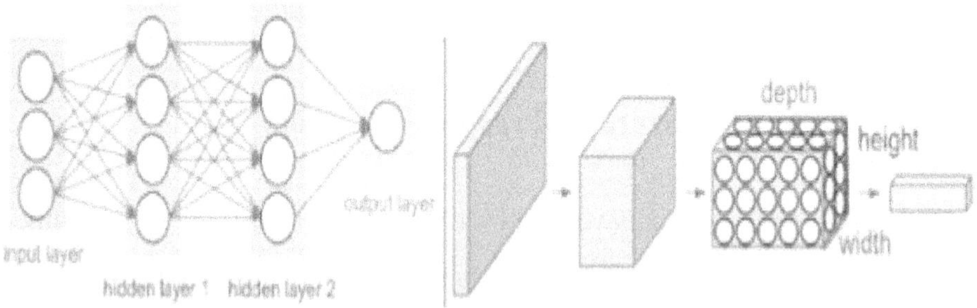

Figure 3.8 An Architecture of Convolutional Neural Network

Table 3.3 Proposed CNN Hyper Parameters

Hyper Parameter	Number of Observations	Range
Number of Filters	3	[16 - 128]
Kernel Size	3	[3, 4, 5]
Hidden Layer	full_hidden	[60, 100, 125]

It is applied in various problems to obtain solutions like classifications, anomaly detection, facial recognition and feature detection (Azmoodeh, *et al.*, 2018). The proposed hyper parameter for the CNN is shown in Table 3.3.

$$\emptyset: X \rightarrow F$$

$$\varphi: F \rightarrow X$$

$$\emptyset, \varphi == \arg\min_{\Phi,\varphi} ||X - (\varphi o\ \emptyset)X||^2$$

Where, X is the input value and Y defines the target value and $\emptyset, \varphi$ are referred as transitions. F is referred as feature space for the input size X and feature vector is represented as $\emptyset$ (x).

E. Model Validation

Proposed DL based model is evaluated from the performance metrics like accuracy, precision, recall and F1 score. Confusion matrix is calculated as the first step of model validation for categorizing the malware and benign samples. True Positive (TP) defines appropriately categorized malwares and True Negative (TN) describes benign samples. False Positive (FP) indicates inappropriate categorization of benign samples and False Negative (FN) signifies inappropriate categorization malware instances.

Accuracy

Accuracy describes proposed model's absolute success rate. It is computed with the comparison of the amount of correctly classified malware and benign incidence to the total incidences.

$$Accuracy = \frac{TP + TN}{TP + TN + FP + FN}$$

Precision

Efficiency of the proposed model is predicted making use of precision. It is computed as the percentage of malicious incidences.

$$Precision = \frac{TP}{TP + FP}$$

Recall

It represents real time malware categorization as percentage to calculate absolute success rate of proposed model.

$$Recall = \frac{TP}{(TP + FN)}$$

F1 score

F1 score is computed with the harmonious mean of precision and recall measures. Accuracy is predicted as statistical function.

$$F1\ score = \frac{2 * TP}{2 * TP + FP + FN}$$

3.3 SECURED IoT MALWARE DETECTION FRAMEWORK USING AI BASED FUZZY LOGIC SYSTEMS

3.3.1 Introduction

IoT security market value is projected as $40.3 billion by the year 2026, while IoT market worth is predicted as $1102.6 billion for the same year on the basis of current research report (Hassan & Wan Haslina 2019), (Sfar *et al.*, 2018). IoT security market is evolved with 22.1% Compound Annual Growth Rate (CAGR) from the year 2021. Google, Microsoft, AWS,

Cisco, IBM, Erickson and Thales plays a key role in the market of IoT security. While considering the application areas of IoT, banking and financial services are on the top of the list following by IT services. It is observed that even healthcare and government related applications also hold more percentage of market value. Massive connectivity through billions of devices in IoT ecosystem requires secure end to end communication without any issues related to security and privacy. McKinsey Global Institute projected that 64 million IoT devices will be used globally in 2025 which implies that per second 127 new connected devices will be available in the IoT ecosystem (Sood, K *et al.,* 2020), (Al-Garadi, MA *et al.,* 2020). Vast utilization of IoT devices lead to the enormous amount of attacks (Granjal, J *et al.,* 2015). It is important to combat strongly against their exploitation to avoid infections. IoT malware detection and prevention mechanisms need to be implemented effectively and efficiently where classical systems failed to fight against advanced malwares and their techniques.

Each and every devices and equipment's in the IoT ecosystem should be switched on for all time which makes attackers easy to investigate power mode of the devices any time. Further, IoT ecosystem is made of interconnected devices and equipment's which will allow attackers accessing through interconnected devices. IoT malwares impair IoT ecosystem because of improper encryption features and weak authentication methods of interconnected devices. In addition all the interconnected devices require full time internet which will allow attackers to perform vulnerable attacks to IoT. Appropriate security measures need to be incorporated in the interconnected devices of IoT for combating against attacks by considering the issues related to security, confidentiality and privacy. Characteristics and attributes of malware may vary for one device and other. IoT applications based cyber-attacks can be either internal attack, external attack or both. Attacker comprises node of the network during inside attack where as in outside attack attacker is out of network. Different types of IoT attacks taxonomy is depicted in Figure 3.9.

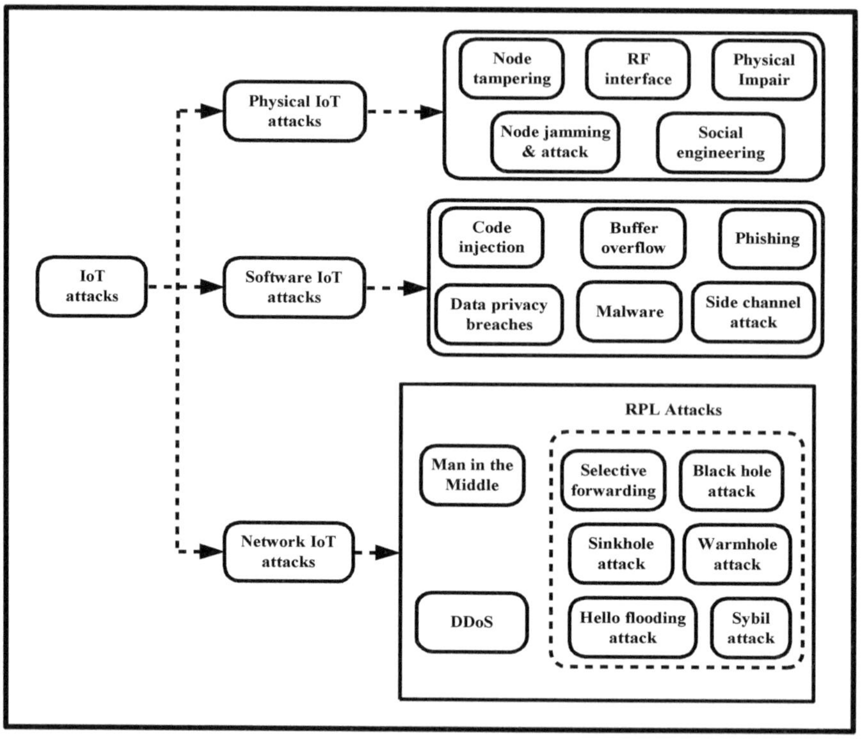

Figure 3.9 Types of IoT Attacks

Based on SonicWall, amount of IoT malware attacks is enlarged by 30% with the size of 32.4 million in 2020 (Meidan, Y *et al.,* 2017). IoT devices require more advancement in security aspect for avoiding IoT attacks. In the mid of 2020, Linux malware Kaiji is identified. It is entirely developed making use of Golang for targeting IoT devices by applying brute force attacks in Secure Shell (SSH). Similarly another malware Mirai is the dangerous one which involves in 40% of malware assaults. In 2016 it is developed by kids for performing online services based DDoS attacks. Self-replication method is used for contaminating IoT devices and their Command and Control (C&C) severs and Industrial IoT is affected heavily with advanced Mirai malwares. Further Mirai botnets are also developed by employing Trojans.

Palo Alto networks identified Muhstik botnet in the beginning of 2020 which implements authentication based brute force attacks towards tomato routers. Likewise another malware MukashiMirai is discovered by the same Palo Alto networks which execute brute force attacks in C&C server. These kinds of IoT malwares are very hazardous which are intended to impair IoT devices and ecosystem. Secured and strong resistance system is required for avoiding and combating against IoT malwares and many security analysts and providers are working on it. Multi factor authentication based security systems are recommended by several analysts.

The key contribution of the work are summarized as below:

- AI based Fuzzy Logic System is utilized for designing the proposed IoT malware detection framework.

- Recent research works on IoT malware detection are studied in detail and the shortcomings are considered for the development of proposed framework.

- Automatic fuzzy rules generation system is implemented for enhancing the effectiveness of the system and it is validated with the performance metrics True Positive Rate (TPR), False Positive Rate (FPR), False Negative Rate (FNR) and Classification Rate (accuracy).

- Fuzzy Pattern Trees are too used for improving detection efficiency of the proposed framework.

3.3.2 Related Work

This section details about the recent research works of IoT malware detection whereas multiple research works are carried in order to ensure the security of IoT devices as well as IoT ecosystem. Summary of the recent research works is presented in Table 3.4. Power consumption prototypes are used for detecting crypto ransom ware in IoT environment along with ML techniques (Iqbal, H *et al.,* 2020). KNN affords better performance in accurately detecting malwares by considering the time and similarity based metrics than other ML techniques like Random Forest, SVM and Neural Networks. Result is shown with 95.65% detection rate and 89.19% precision.

Deep Eigen space learning based IoT and Internet of Battlefield Things (IoBT) malware detection method is proposed (Jeon, J *et al.,* 2020). Operational code (Opcode) sequence of the devices are utilized and they are converted into vector space. Graph is generated using selected features. Afterwards deep Eigen space learning technique is applied for classifying malwares and benign files. As per experimented results, 99.68% accuracy, 98.59% precision and 98.37% recall are attained. To detect IoT malwares effectively, dynamic programming algorithm is proposed on the basis of control flow features (9). It concentrates on polynomial time O($N2$) in which N describes basic blocks of decompiled exe codes. While applying this algorithm in IoT datasets, better results are achieved which are 99.05% accuracy, 1.31% TPR and 0.66% TNR.

Blockchain and ML techniques are combined to detect android IoT malwares. Malware information is extracted using clustering and classification methods of ML and block chain is used for information storing (Sudhakaran & Pradeep 2021). Clustering algorithm enhance feature selection by computing weights for every feature set, developing optimized parametric study and reducing unwanted features repeatedly. Multi-purpose Naive Bayes classifier is used for classification purpose with more accuracy. 98% accuracy is achieved with 0.98 F measure according to the results.

In information centric IoT environment Advanced Persistent Threats detection scheme is proposed making use of domain graphs (https://www.marketsandmarkets.com). Relations between malicious domains and their corresponding IP addresses are discovered. Subgraphs with more links are incorporated for acquiring domain graph. Dataset of 257535071 DNS requests and 73136 domain names is processed to analyses the performance.

Intelligent and dynamic analysis based IoT malware detection scheme is proposed in order to detect familiar as well as novel IoT malwares (https://cybersecurity.att.com). Convolution Neural Network (CNN) model is utilized for performing dynamic analysis in the IoT environment. Feature extraction involves with the features like network, memory, process, system call and Virtual File System (VFS). Behavioral images sof IoT malwares are generated after converting extracted behavior data. CNN model is trained with the behavioral images of malwares. Based on the experimental results, 99.28% accuracy is attained.

ML methods are utilized for effective malware detection and classification. Byte sequences of executable program files are discovered for detection as well as classification (Akram, H *et al.,* 2018). With the 7 CPU architectures, large sized dataset is utilized which is comprised with 111K benign samples and 111K malware samples. Experimental results are depicted with 99.96% accuracy and 98.47% accuracy for malware detection and malware family classification respectively. Further, Support Vector Machine (SVM) is combined for enhancing performance.

Two level IoT malware detection mechanism is proposed by considering node level and network level (https://www.trgdatacenters.com). Light weighted runtime malware detector is deployed at node level to detect malwares which utilizes Hardware Performance Counter (HPC) values. Information of node level malware and malware propagation are combined together without obstructing the performance of network. In addition, multi-attribute graph translation is proposed to range and predict the topology size of network and it attained 5.88 Root Mean Square Error (RMSE).

RGB images based feature representation technique is applied for proposing enhanced malware visualization scheme for detecting IoT malwares making use of CNN (https://www.globalsign.com). Created image includes information of binary, assembly and string. CNN model is utilized for combining self-attention mechanism with spatial pyramid pooling. Spatial pyramid pooling helps in avoiding information loss though IoT files are received in various sizes and it increases detection accuracy and efficiency. For experimental purpose above 10K malware samples of 25 families are utilized and 98.57% accuracy achieved.

Large scale IoT malware and family classification is performed on the basis of characteristics and relationships among malwares (Melamed, T 2018). More than 70K recent malware executable files including COVID – 19 related malware samples are utilized for analysis purpose. Multi-level strings based similarity analysis technique is applied for classification by considering difficulties in binary obfuscation of malwares. Features such as rival IP addresses and malware specific strings are considered for performing reverse engineering.

Industrial Internet of Things (IIoT) malware detection architecture Fed-IIoT is presented which is based on federated learning (Ahmed, M & Pathan, ASK 2020). Fed-IIoT concentrated in the detection of malicious android applications of IIoT. It is included with 2 parts which are participant and server. In participant part, data triggering is performed with 2 dynamic poisoning attacks on the basis of Generative Adversarial Network (GAN) and Federated Generative Adversarial Network (FedGAN). In server part, global model monitoring and robust training model modeling are aimed for avoiding A3GAN (anomaly in aggregation by GAN network). Fed-IIoT ensures secure communication without privacy related issues. Proposed method is validated with 3 IoT datasets. It is observed that Fed-IIoT provides 8% better accuracy than earlier methods.

DL based multi-dimensional classification approach is proposed to secure future networks like 5G by considering the issues of IoT malware obfuscation (http://www.trend micro .com). For feature extraction executable binary files are represented in strings and image formats. More than 70 thousand samples of IoT malware are analyzed and 99.78% accuracy is achieved for familiar malware families. Further for unknown malware samples, IoT tailored method is used.

Table 3.4 Summary of Recent Works

Research	Features	Proposed Model/Algorithm	Performance results
Dib *et al.*, (2021)	Binary files, IoT tailored method	DL based multi-dimensional classification approach	99.78% accuracy
Taheri *et al.*, (2021)	Federated learning, FedGAN	Fed-IIoT	8% better accuracy
Torabi *et al.*, (2021)	Characteristics and relationships amid malwares	Multi level Strings-Based Similarity Analysis Approach	86.6% detection
Li *et al.*, (2021)	RGB images, binary, assembly and string	CNN	98.57% accuracy

	information		
Dinakarrao *et al.*, (2020)	HPC values, multi-attribute graph translation	Two level IoT malware detection	5.88 RMSE
Wan *et al.*, (2020)	7 CPU architectures, Byte sequences of exe.	ML, SVM	99.96% accuracy for malware, 98.47% accuracy for malware family
Jeon *et al.*, (2020)	Network, memory, process, system call and VFS, Behavioural images	CNN	99.28% accuracy
Ma *et al.*, (2019)	IP address, APT detection in IoT, Domain graph	Large-Scale Domain Graph	257535071 DNS requests and 73136 domain names
Kumar *et al.*, (2019)	Android malware in IoT, block chain & ML	Multi-purpose Naive Bayes	98% accuracy, 0.98 F measure
NghiPhu *et al.*, (2019)	Control flow features, polynomial time	Dynamic programming	99.05% accuracy, 1.31% TPR and 0.66% TNR
Azmoodeh *et al.*, (2018)	Sequence of opcodes, IoT and IoBT malware	Deep Eigen space learning	99.68% accuracy, 98.59% precision and 98.37% recall
Azmoodeh *et al.*, (2018)	Power consumption prototypes	KNN	95.65% detection rate and 89.19% precision

3.3.3 AI based Fuzzy Logic Systems

Fuzzy logic system is based on rules which in the form of multiple values where, the truth values related to the variables lie amid 0 and 1. It will be considered as AI's subset and applied mainly for decision making process. In real time environment, there will be some complicated situations where unable to state if it is true or false. In such situation, fuzzy logic makes decision making simple. Truth values of Boolean system are displayed with fixed truth value 1 and false value 0 where, as in fuzzy logic system no logic is applied for fixed truth and false value and it is comprised with in between values which are utilized for displaying partial true and false values. Further in fuzzy logic system, membership functions are utilized for mapping values in between 0 and 1 with graph representation.

Fuzzy logic algorithm considers all the offered data for resolving problem. Further, finest feasible decision is obtained from the specified input. FL resembles the decision making process of human being which focuses each and every possibilities amid T value and F value. Fuzzy logic concept is learned from 1920s and its term is initially used by LotfiZadeh in the year 1965 where conventional computer logic is observed for data manipulation.

While considering the characteristics of Fuzzy Logic, it seems flexible for machine learning, resembles human decision process, two valued solution representation, appropriate for approximate reasoning and permits to develop nonlinear functions. Fuzzy Logic System is designed with four important components which are depicted in Figure 3.10.

Rule Base: It includes all rules where, experts offer conditions on the basis of If-Then to influence decision making process. Recent fuzzy theory offer several techniques to design and altering fuzzy controllers. This updated system decreases the number of rule sets.

Fuzzification: Inputs are converted in fuzzification stage. Crisp numbers are transferred into fuzzy sets. After that computed crisp inputs of sensors are conceded towards control system.

Inference Engine: It facilitates the selection of appropriate match amid rules and fuzzy input. Match is measured in terms of % and based on that, rules to be implemented are decided for the input given. Then related rules are integrated for developing control actions.

Defuzzification: It is the last stage where, fuzzy sets are converted into crisp values by using various available methods. Based on the requirements suitable techniques are utilized by an expert system

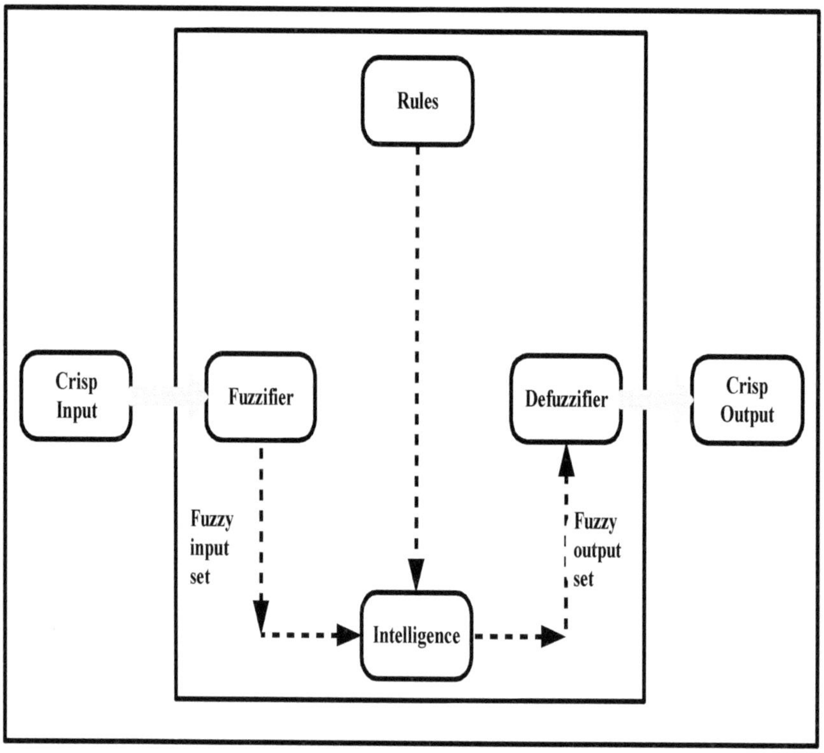

Figure 3.10 Fuzzy Logic System

Fuzzy logic systems provides simple understanding, accurate reasoning, controls machines, highly robust and effectively resolves complex issues. Further, it is applied into various fields like anti-lock brakes, auto transmission, auto engine, dishwasher, elevator control, microwave oven, fitness management, palmtop computer, plasma catching and so on by the various familiar companies like Nissan, Canon, Honda, Matsushita, Fujitec, Mitsubishi Electric, Toshiba and others.

3.3.4 Proposed Framework

Comprehensive view of proposed IoT malware detection framework is presented in this section. It also includes the details of utilized datasets and performance metrics utilized for validating security performance. Input of the framework includes both benign and malware files.

A. Proposed Framework

Proposed framework is categorized into various stages which are debugging; feature processing, feature selection and classification. Introduce an information system with decision attribute. Eliminate information system inconsistency, i.e., objects with the same information function values, but different decision values, applying lower or upper approximation precision analysis. Apply rule induction and define rules for all considered decisions, which cover the decision problem. It is portrayed in Figure 3.11 and the important components of framework are explained as follows.

Debugging

UNSW-NB15 and Bot-IoT datasets are used in which 80% of records of both datasets are applied for training and remaining 20% records of both datasets are utilized for validating the proposed framework. It will help to analyses and train the behavioral features of IoT malwares. IoT malware detection is performed by executing all the executable files in real time environment which includes both benign and malware samples. After that debugging is performed over the accomplished files.

Feature Processing

After debugging step, feature processing is implemented. Feature processing is performed in two stages which are feature preprocessing and feature extraction. Feature preprocessing involves cleansing of unwanted or not required features for malware detection. During feature extraction all the available behavioural features are analysed for IoT malwares from the datasets provided by considering all the attributes of both benign files and malware files. Output of feature processing is forwarded as the input for feature selection.

Feature Selection and Classification

In feature selection, appropriate feature is selected for categorizing benign and malware files in IoT ecosystem. AI based Fuzzy Logic System (AIFLS) and Fuzzy Pattern Tree (FPT) are utilized in feature selection and classification stage to improve detection rate effectively.

AI based Fuzzy logic systems

AIFLS is a rules based system used for effective decision making. Automated fuzzy rules generation is implemented with effective learning. Fuzzy rules are provided by experts by analyzing the malicious behaviors usually and for large scaled data with more attributes, it is hard to define fuzzy rules manually. One length of frequent items of attributes are identified from utilized UNSW-NB15 and Bot-IoT datasets making use of Apriori mining algorithm by considering only two classes benign and malware. Appropriate attribute selection of rule generation is implemented because all attributes need not to be utilized for effective detection. Suitable attribute selection will enhance the process of classifying benign and malicious records. Deviation method is utilized for suitable attribute identification by using one length frequent items. One length frequent items of every attribute are carried as a vector of two classes (i.e class 1 for benign and class 2 for malware) and it is defined as

$$C_i=(V_1, V_2, \ldots. V_n)$$

Where for benign, i is assigned as 1 and for malware i is assigned as 2. Every vector (Vj) includes frequent items and frequency should be maximum than minimum support. $V_j=\{f_i;1<=i<=m\};support(f_i)>=min\_support$. Afterwards for every attribute, frequent item's deviation range {max, min} is computed by performing the comparison in available frequent items of vector and it is formulated as follows.

$$D_{v(j)}=\{f_{max}, f_{min}\} \text{ where } f_{max}=Max(fj) \text{ and } f_{min}=Min(fj)$$

For identifying appropriate attribute, one to one comparison is applied for both max and min classes. Attributes without similar range are selected for appropriate attribute which will improvise the detection and classification of the system. Appropriate attribute selection is defined as follows

$$C^i=(V^{(1)}, V^{(2)}, V^{(3)}, \ldots. V^{(j)}, \ldots V^{(k)}) \text{ where } k<=n$$

During rule generation, valuable attributes selected from earlier stage are used which are resultant of {max, min} deviation. Deviation range is compared amid benign and malicious data and intersection points are discovered.

Definite and indefinite rules are developed using two intersection points. If-Then condition is applied for deciding whether the data is benign or attack. Based on range various rule are generated and in some cases two rules only generated. Generated rules are filtered for effective designing of classification system by considering two conditions.

First condition is about reducing more number of possible fuzzy rules where second condition is about shortening if section in fuzzy rules. Definite rules are used for making fuzzy rules numerical variables of definite rules are fuzzified. So that effectiveness of the proposed system is improved.

To find a suitable classification from test input, test dataset is provided for developed fuzzy logic system. Fuzzifier transfers attributes as linguistic variable making use of triangular membership function. Resultant of fuzzifier is provided for inference engine which evaluates specified input using rule base. Rule base is defined as knowledge base which includes set of rules acquire by definite rules.

Outcome of inference engine is in the form of linguistic values with the set {Low & High} after that defuzzifier coverts into crisp values. Crisp value of fuzzy inference engine is ranged from 0 to 1 where '0' defines data as entirely benign and '1' defines data as entirely malicious.

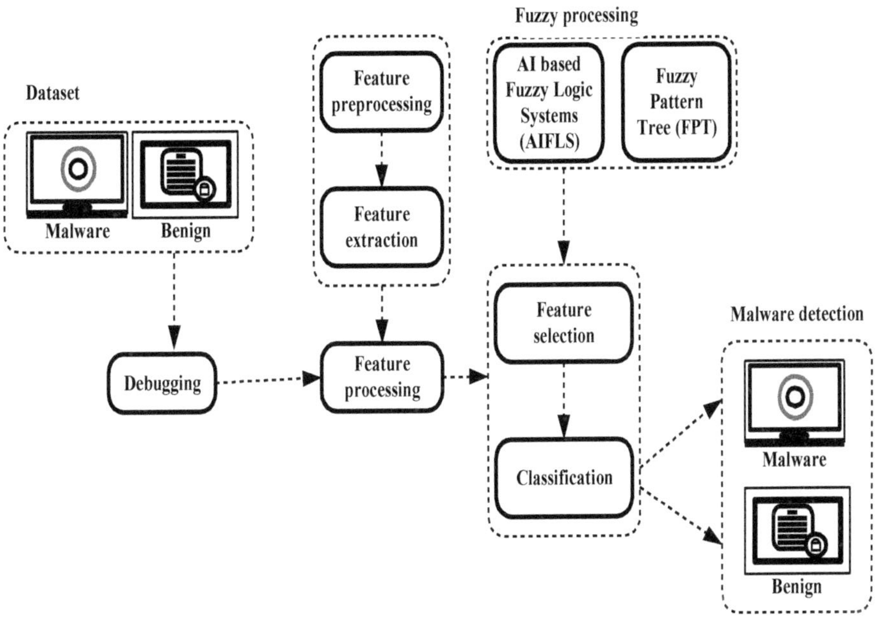

Figure 3.11 Proposed Framework

Fuzzy Pattern Tree (FPT)

Fuzzy pattern tree is also employed for fastening IoT malware detection effectively. It is included with a tree like structure where fuzzy logic arithmetic operators are considered as inner nodes and input attribute based fuzzy predicates are considered as leaf nodes (Stone, J 2019). Fuzzy pattern tree is depicted in Figure 3.12. Bottom up induction is applied for fuzzy pattern tree in which values of leaf nodes are combined making use of fuzzy operators. At the end, output is presented to its ancestor. Various pattern trees are created in every iteration while implementing iterative method. Pattern tree with minimum prediction error is considered as best pattern tree. Datasets are applied with fuzzy pattern tree for IoT malware detection with instance vector $X=(x_1,x_2,\ldots\ldots,x_n) \in X_1xX_2x\ldots xX_n$ where X_i is defined as the ith attribute of every domain.

Fuzzy partition F_i is described by descretizing the value of X_i which is defined as $F_i=\{F_{(I,1)},\dots F_{(I,di)}\}$ and fuzzy subset $F_{i,j}$ is defined as $F_{i,j}=Xi\rightarrow(0,1)$ $(j=1,\dots.di)$ and $\sum_{j=1}^{di} Fi,j(xi)$ for all x ϵ X_i. $F_{i,j}$ describes the unary fuzzy predicator as attribute which are defined with the labels 'large' or 'small'. On other side, every instance is also related with label benign or malware for output space Y {benign, malware}. Fuzzy partition $F_{i,j}$ links each and every leaf nodes.

Fuzzy pattern classifier is defined as a set of Fuzzy Pattern Trees (FPT). FPT is defined as FPT = {FPTi|i =1,..,k} and every FPT_i is related with class yiϵ Y. To classify fresh instance x, prediction is done on the basis of class of the tree with maximum score which is defined as follows

$y^{\wedge} = argmax(PTi(x))$ *for* $y_i \epsilon Y$

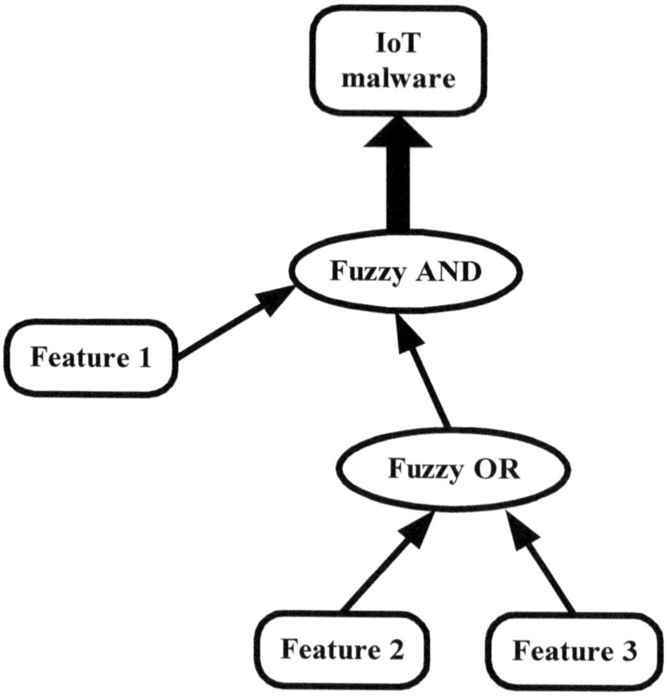

Figure 3.12 Fuzzy Pattern Tree

Prediction error of a pattern tree at every iteration is computed for selecting best pattern tree. It is computed as follows

$$error(FPTz) = 1/N \sqrt{\sum_{j=1}^{N} (y^j - PTz(x^j))}$$

B. Datasets Utilized

UNSW-NB15 and Bot-IoT datasets are utilized for the proposed IoT malware detection framework. UNSW-NB15 dataset contains 2,57,673 data records which is based on network intrusions (20). Further, it describes about nine different attacks including trojans, DDoS, DoS, worms, backdoors and fuzzers.

Bot-IoT dataset is related to real time dynamic network environment. It is included with 72000000 records and size of Bot-IoT dataset is 69.3 GB of pcap files. It is available in csv format too for downloading in 16.7 GB size. DDoS, DoS, OS and service scan, data exfiltration and key logging are the different types of included attacks of the dataset.

3.4 SUMMARY

This chapter summarizes the various proposed schemes for securing IoT framework, which are discussed. The chapter exhibits three novel schemes and all the schemes are effective and outperforms the existing state of the art methods. Out of the proposed schemes, the scheme, which utilizes AI based logics, outperforms other two schemesss in terms of accuracy and performance. Furthermore, all the schemes are validated in real time. A detailed experimental setup for each methodology is given in the Chapter 4.

CHAPTER 4

RESULTS AND DISCUSSION

The proposed schemes are experimentally validated in real time. All the three schemes test bed, experimental setup, results and discussions are clearly given in this chapter.

4.1 AN INTELLIGENT IoT ATTACK DETECTION FRAMEWORK USING EFFECTIVE EDGE AI BASED COMPUTING

Experimental Setup and Results

UNSW-NB15 is utilized for both training and testing processes which is set of core network packets. For training 1,75,341 records are utilized while for testing 82,332 records are used in terms of various types of attack and normal types. Almost 70% of data samples are used for training phase and the balance 30% of data samples are utilized for testing phase.

Training and testing phase utilize the optimized feature set after edge-computing phase as input set. Both training and testing are implemented based on signatures, anomalies and abnormal behaviors respectively. Attack signatures are meant by malicious patterns which are obtained by continuously monitoring inbound and outbound network traffic. Indicators of Compromise (IoCs) is utilized for signatures related to attack behaviors, recognized byte sequences and file hashes. There are various shortcomings regarding to signatures which are lack in the detection of unknown attacks. Encrypted traffic and altered attack pattern may also unable to detect while using signatures. To overcome those limitations in this proposed framework anomalies and abnormal behaviors also taken for training and testing additionally.

Anomalies are applied for training phase to test behavioral patterns in abnormal manner. Naïve Bayes classifier model is utilized for recovering from the limitations of signatures. Mainly it is used for detecting unknown attacks. Naïve Bayes is probabilistic model which is familiar for classification. Bayes theorem is root of Naïve Bayes classifier model which is also utilized. Figures 4.1 – 4.4 shows the performance results of the given dataset.

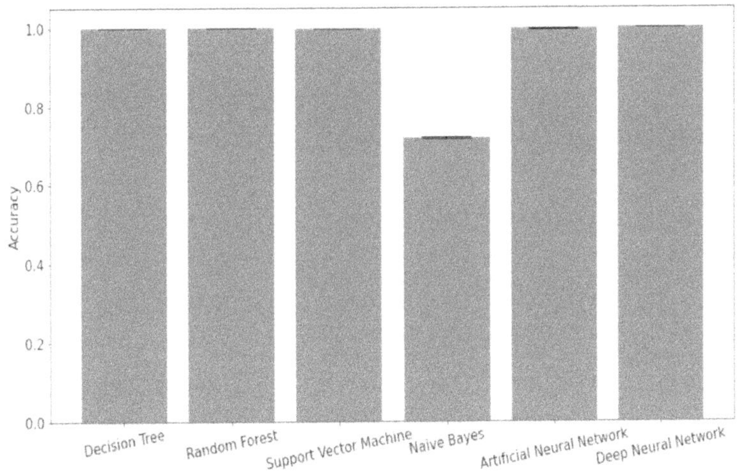

Figure 4.1 Performance Results – Accuracy

```
------------------------- Decision Tree -------------------------
Accuracy: [0.9994506  0.99927062 0.99937482 0.99944112 0.99947901]
mean: 0.9994             std: 0.0001
------------------------- Random Forest -------------------------
Accuracy: [0.99947901 0.99939376 0.99948849 0.99955479 0.99950743]
mean: 0.9995             std: 0.0001
------------------------- Support Vector Machine ----------------------
Accuracy: [0.9961447  0.99604998 0.9962489  0.99560477 0.99543422]
mean: 0.9959             std: 0.0003
------------------------- Naive Bayes -------------------------
Accuracy: [0.72010723 0.71536152 0.72096922 0.72336576 0.71898681]
mean: 0.7198             std: 0.0026
------------------------- Artificial Neural Network -------------------
Accuracy: [0.9953206  0.99603103 0.99587    0.99562372 0.99524477]
mean: 0.9956             std: 0.0003
------------------------- Deep Neural Network -------------------------
Accuracy: [0.99842757 0.9983139  0.99826654 0.99867385 0.99856017]
mean: 0.9984             std: 0.0002
```

(a)

------------------------- Decision Tree -------------------------

	precision	recall	f1-score	support
benign	0.9996	0.9993	0.9994	52627
malicious	0.9993	0.9996	0.9994	52942
accuracy			0.9994	105569
macro avg	0.9994	0.9994	0.9994	105569
weighted avg	0.9994	0.9994	0.9994	105569

------------------------- Random Forest -------------------------

	precision	recall	f1-score	support
benign	0.9995	0.9993	0.9994	52627
malicious	0.9993	0.9995	0.9994	52942
accuracy			0.9994	105569
macro avg	0.9994	0.9994	0.9994	105569
weighted avg	0.9994	0.9994	0.9994	105569

(b)

------------------------- Support Vector Machine ----------

	precision	recall	f1-score	support
benign	0.9954	0.9957	0.9956	52627
malicious	0.9958	0.9954	0.9956	52942
accuracy			0.9956	105569
macro avg	0.9956	0.9956	0.9956	105569
weighted avg	0.9956	0.9956	0.9956	105569

------------------------- Naive Bayes -------------------------

	precision	recall	f1-score	support
benign	0.9600	0.4732	0.6339	52627
malicious	0.6518	0.9804	0.7830	52942
accuracy			0.7276	105569
macro avg	0.8059	0.7268	0.7085	105569
weighted avg	0.8055	0.7276	0.7087	105569

(c)

------------------------- Artificial Neural Network -----------

	precision	recall	f1-score	support
benign	0.9953	0.9967	0.9960	52627
malicious	0.9967	0.9953	0.9960	52942
accuracy			0.9960	105569
macro avg	0.9960	0.9960	0.9960	105569
weighted avg	0.9960	0.9960	0.9960	105569

------------------------- Deep Neural Network -----------------

	precision	recall	f1-score	support
benign	0.9978	0.9985	0.9982	52627
malicious	0.9985	0.9978	0.9982	52942
accuracy			0.9982	105569
macro avg	0.9982	0.9982	0.9982	105569
weighted avg	0.9982	0.9982	0.9982	105569

(d)

Figure 4.2 Performance Results Standard Deviation and Mean

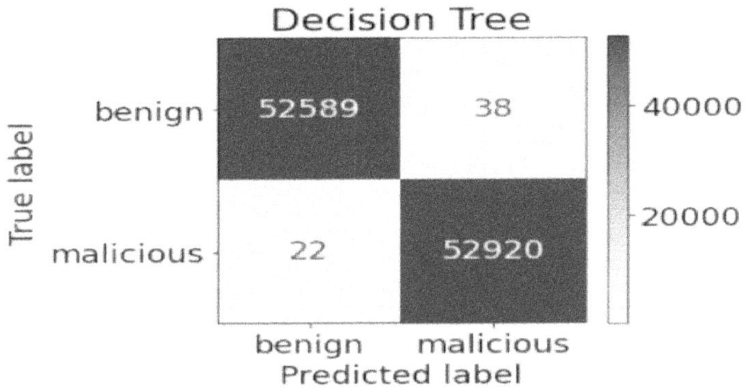

(a) Decision Tree

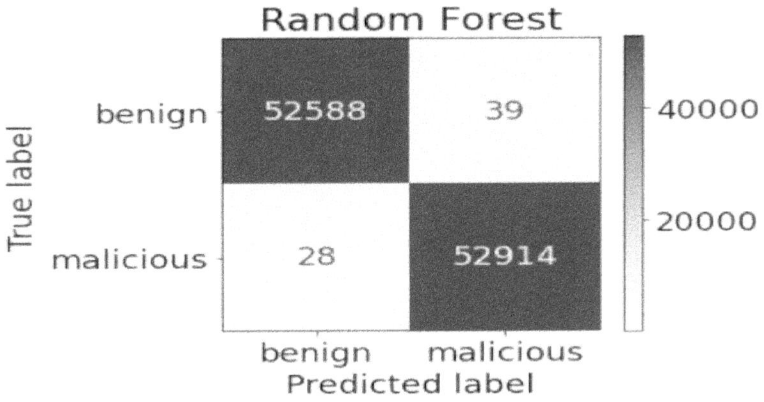

(b) Random Forest

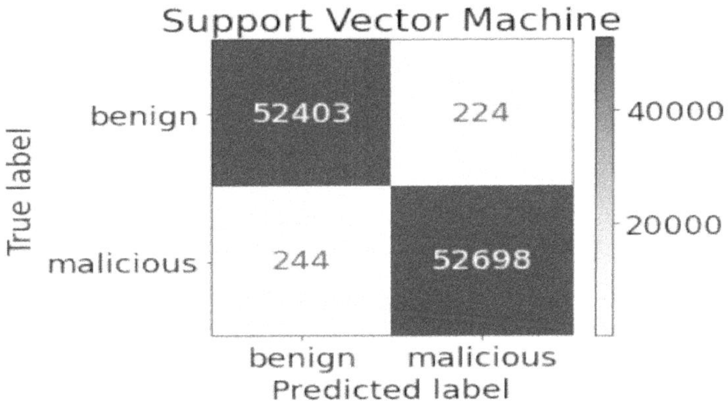

(c) Support Vector Machine

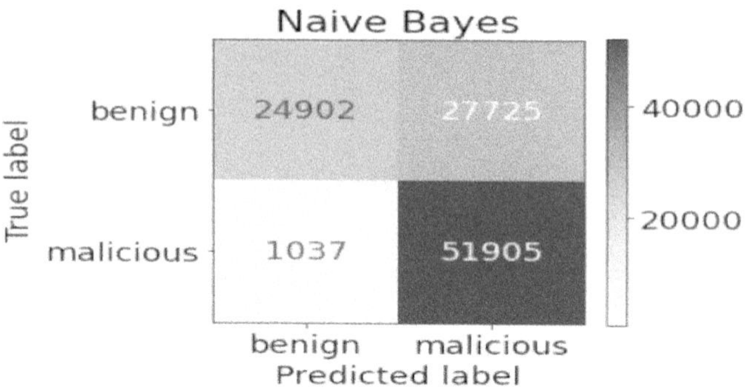

(d) Naïve Bayes

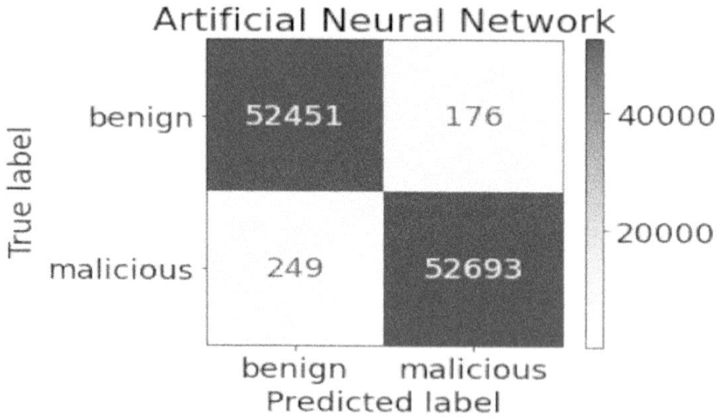

(e) Artificial Neural Network

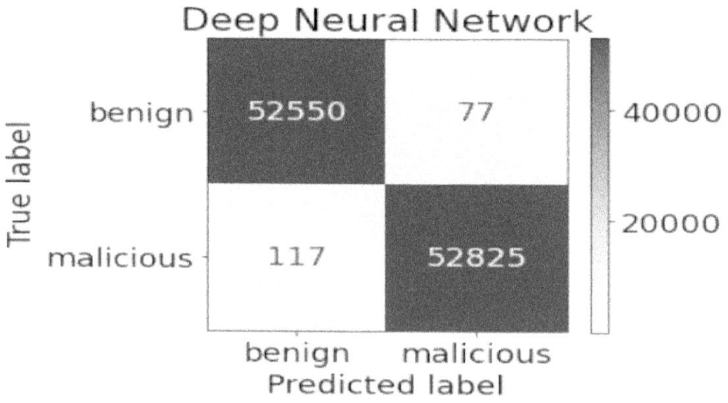

(f) Deep Neural Network

Figure 4.3 Confusion Matrix for Various Classifiers

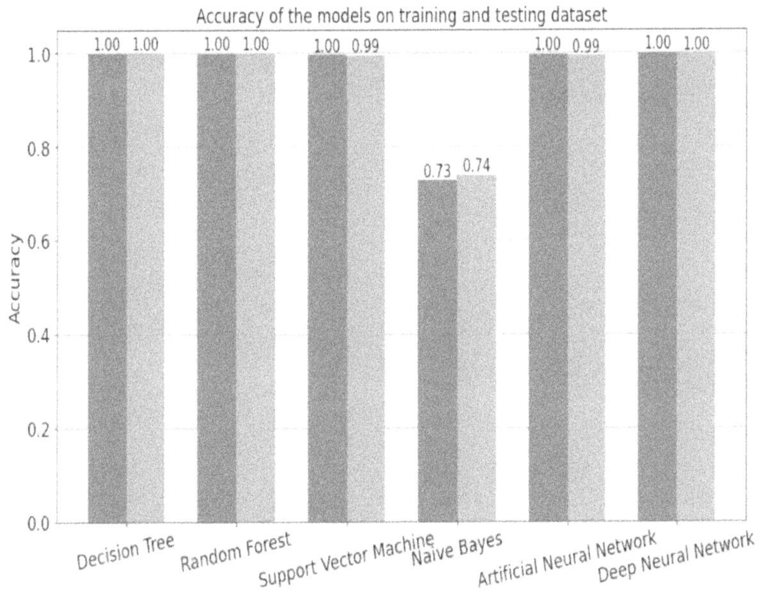

(a) Accuracy of the models on training and testing dataset

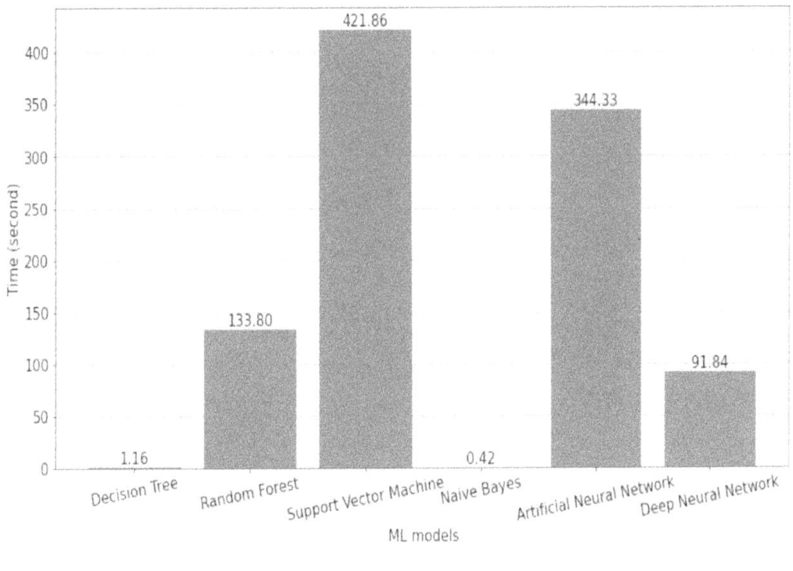

(b) Time Consumption on Training

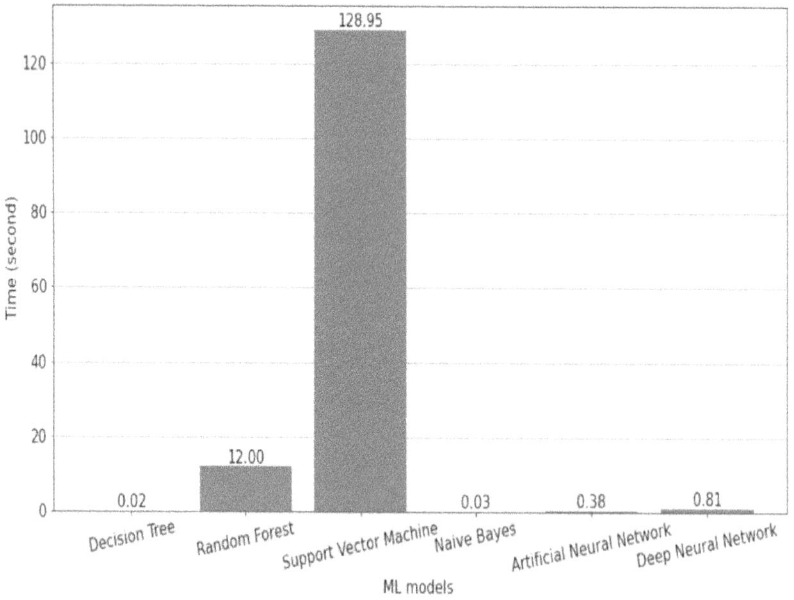

(c) Time Consumption on Testing

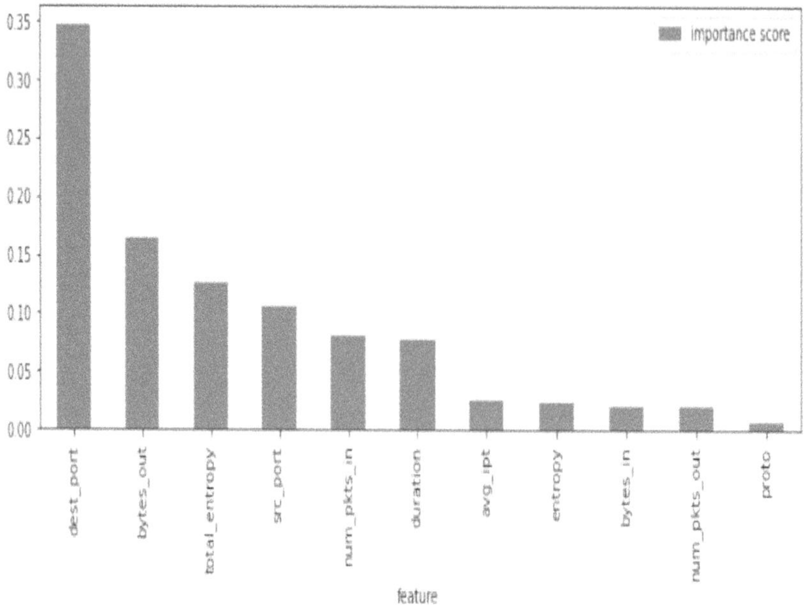

(d) Top Features vs Score (UNSW-NB15 dataset)

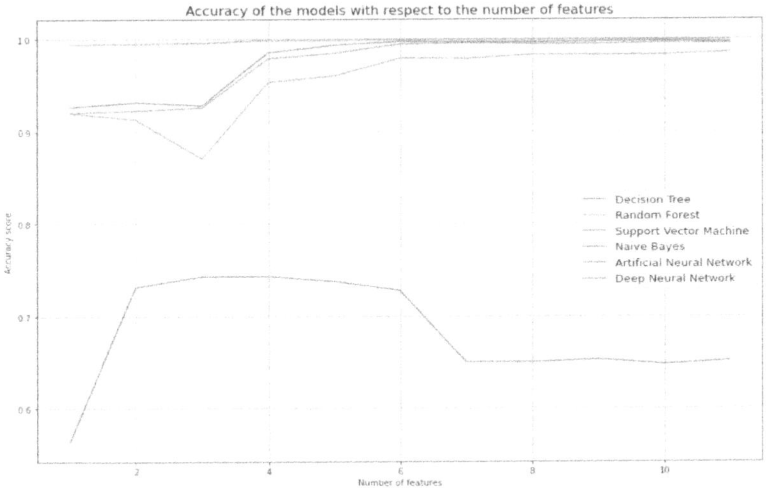

(e) Accuracy of the Models with respect to the Number of Features

Figure 4.4 Training and Testing Metrics

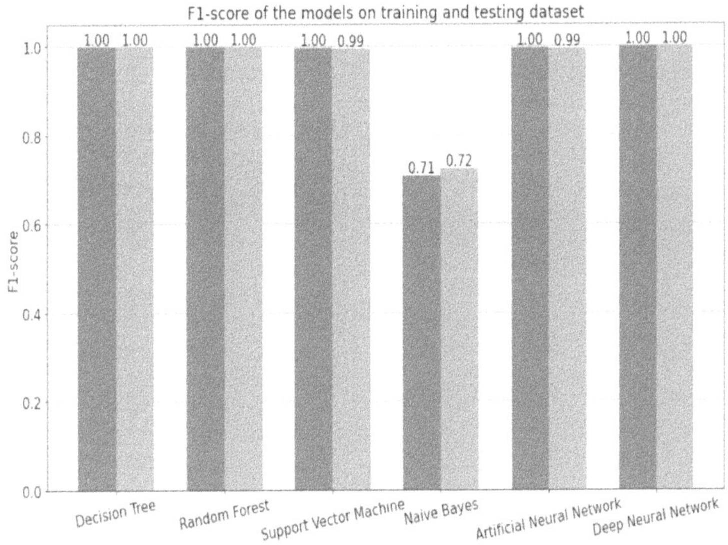

Figure 4.5 F1 Score Training and Testing

Similarly to enhance the detection accuracy, abnormal behaviors of network traffic is also monitored and analyzed other than signatures and anomalies. For observing and analyzing abnormal behaviors in both training and testing phases, AdaBoost M2 algorithm is utilized. For multi-class classification solutions, AdaBoost M1 and Ada Boost M2 models are utilized. AdaBoost M2 overcomes the shortcomings related to the maximized classification errors of Ada Boost M2.

Validation

It is the final phase of proposed framework which discovers intrusion and alert end devices based on the comprehensive processing of previous phases. All types of intrusions are analyzed from UNSW-NB15 dataset. Figure 4.5 shows the experimental results in terms of performance measure such as accuracy and F1-score.

4.2 AN AUTOMATED SECURITY MODEL FOR DATA DRIVEN IoT ECOSYSTEM

The model used in this work is optimal and as per the claim the model achives an accuracy of 99% in overall when compared to the training process. Figure 4.6 shows the training accuracy of the proposed model.

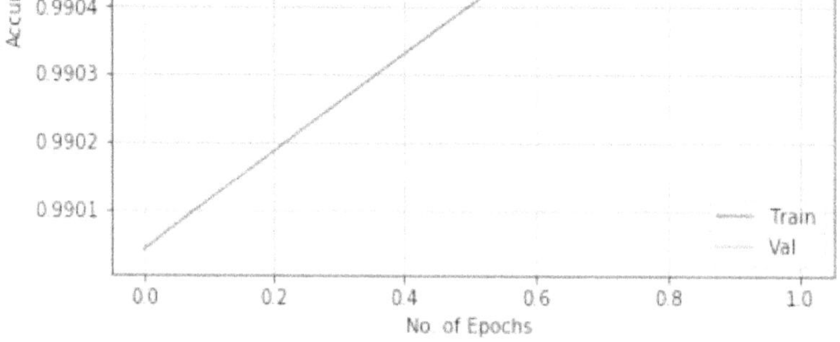

Figure 4.6 Training Accuracy of the Proposed Model

The learning rate is fixed to 0.001 for learning the significant features in the given dataset. The various ROC curves are plotted to understand the train, test and validation which is shown in Figure 4.7. Also, the cross validation score is estimated to understand the maximum threshold to classify the anomaly. Figure 4.8 shows the cross validation plot.

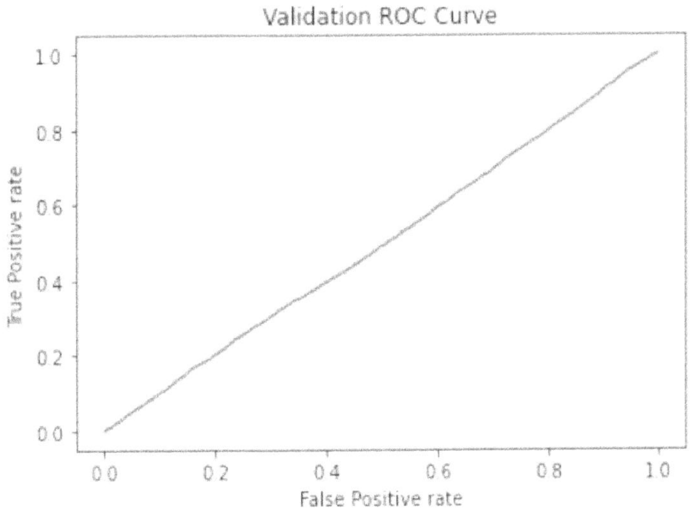

(a) Validation ROC Curve

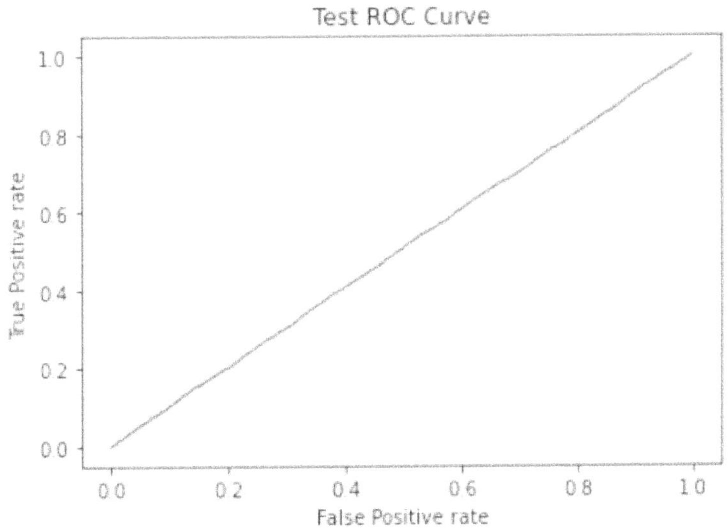

(b) Test ROC Curve

Figure 4.7 Validation and Test Plot

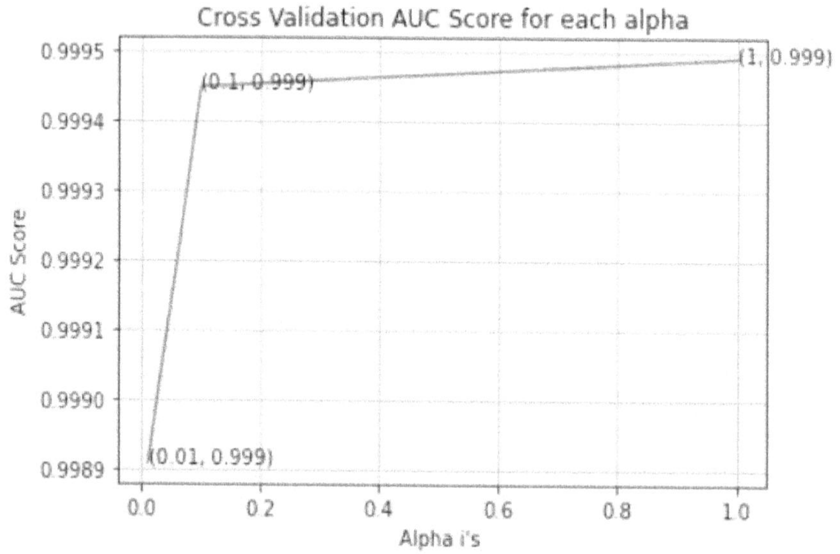

(a) Cross Validation AUC Score for each alpha

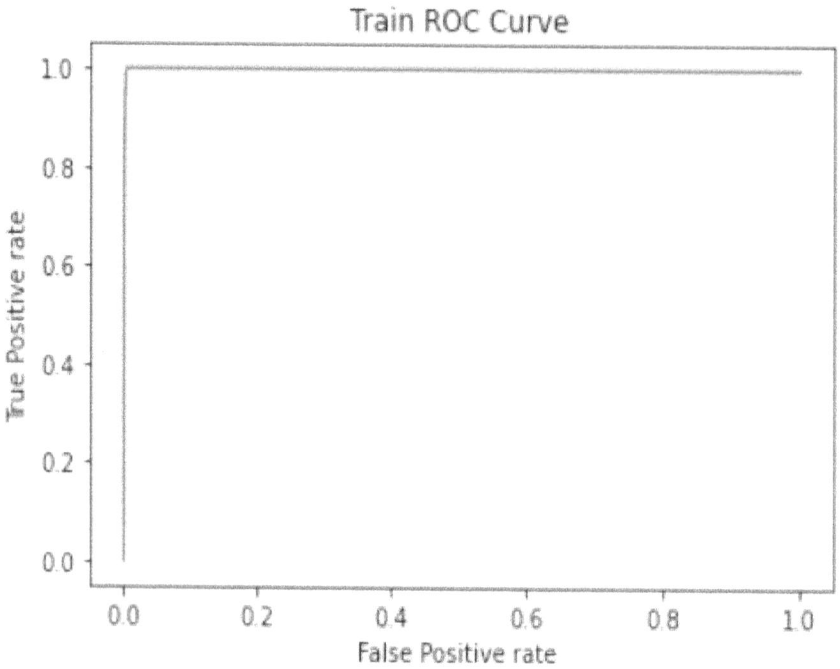

(b) Train ROC Curve

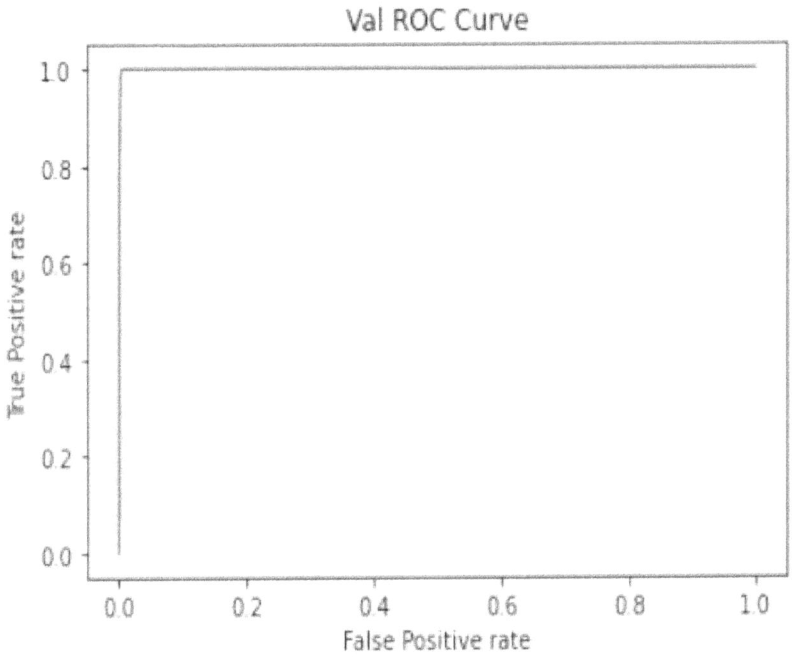

(c) Val ROC Curve

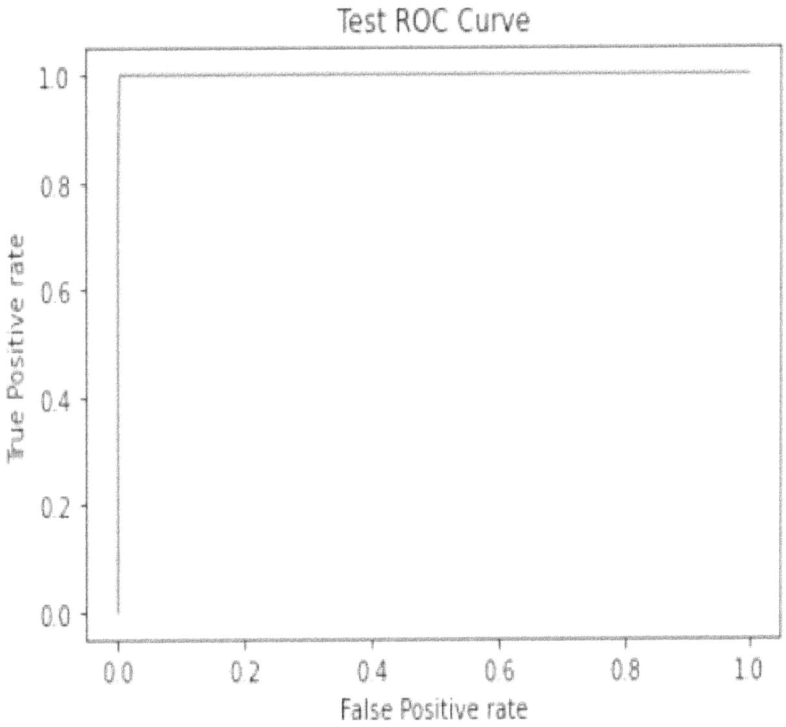

(d) Test ROC Curve

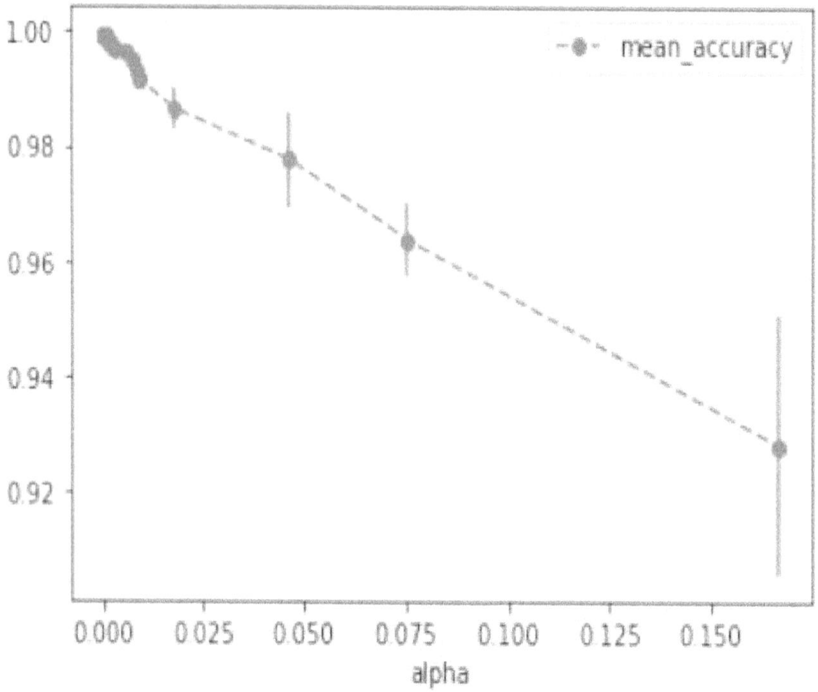

(e) Mean and S.D of the Scores for Each Candidate (UNSW-NB15 dataset)

Figure 4.8 Training, Testing and Cross-Validation Plot

4.3 SECURED IoT MALWARE DETECTION FRAMEWORK USING AI BASED FUZZY LOGIC SYSTEMS

Experimental Setup and Results

The proposed framework is experimentally tested in a secured lab setup carried out in our university. The server runs in Ubuntu server automated using kubernetes for deployment. The kubernetes is configured to automate the data processing and deployment. The experimental validation is performed in the basis of two situation 1) with malware-executed environment and 2) without malware execution.

Figure 4.9 shows the mean and S.D score of the each candidate in the BoT-IoT dataset. Figure 4.10 depicts the top feature score in Bot-IoT dataset. Figure 4.11 and 4.12 shows the performance plot of the proposed scheme.

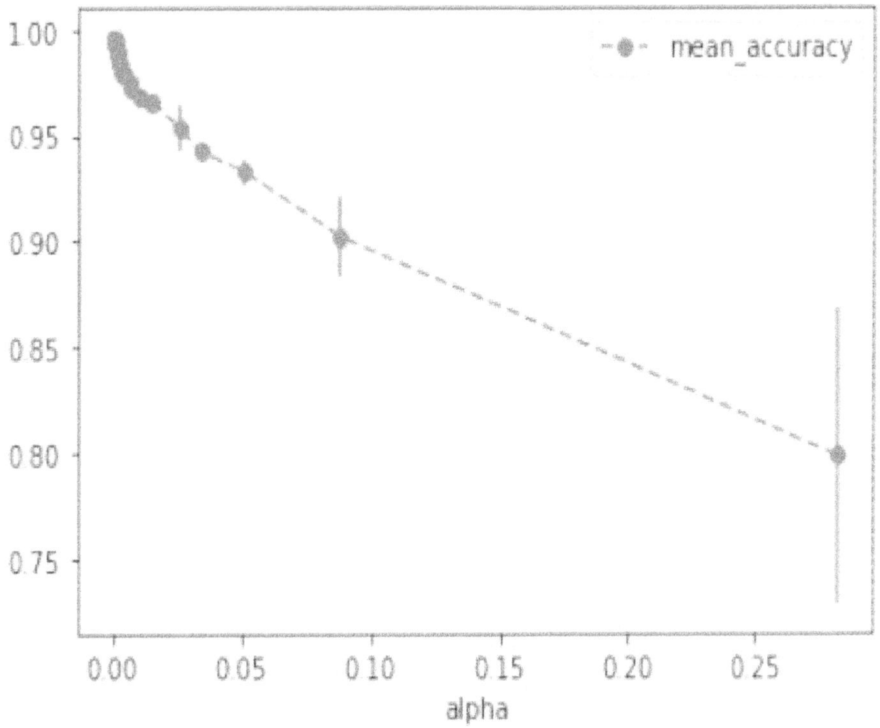

Figure 4.9 Mean and S.D of the Scores for Each Candidate (Bot-IoT Dataset)

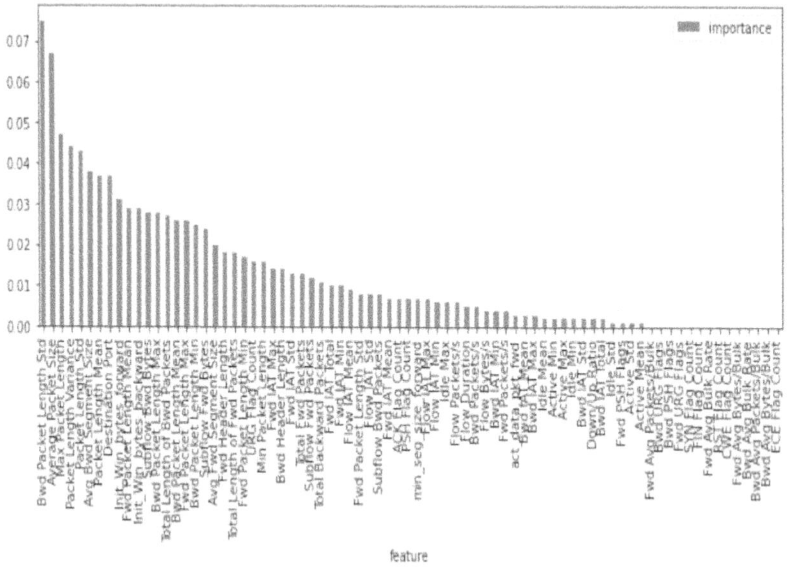

Figure 4.10 Top Features vs Score (Bot-IoT dataset)

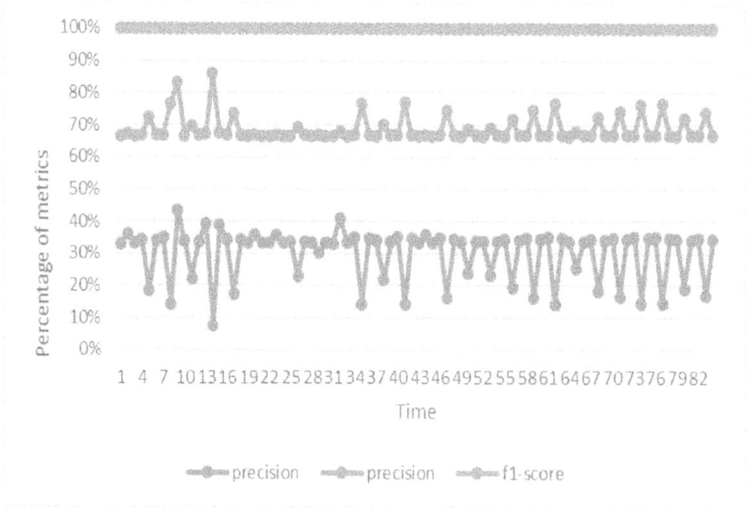

Figure 4.11 Performance Metrics of the Proposed Model (Iteration 1)

Security Validation

Proposed framework is validated with the following performance metrics TPR, FPR, FNR and classification rate.

True Positive Rate (TPR)

It is computed with the ratio amid appropriately forecasted IoT malware count and completely predicted IoT malware count. TPR value will be 1 while all the malwares are detected and it is very rare. TPR is called in other words as the Sensitivity or Detection Rate (DR). It is formulated as follows:

$$TPR = \frac{TP}{TP + FN}$$

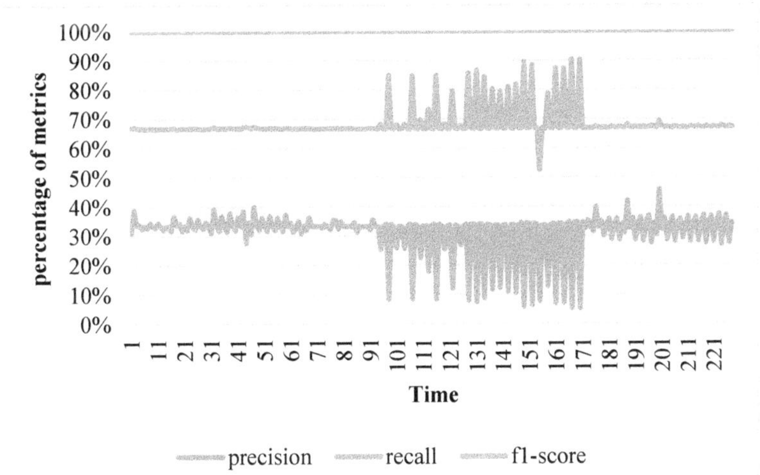

Figure 4.12 Performance Metrics of the Proposed Model (Iteration 2)

False Positive Rate (FPR)

It is computed with the ratio amid the number of benign samples wrongly classified like an attack and the total number of benign samples. It is formulated as follows:

$$FPR = \frac{FP}{FP + TN}$$

False Negative Rate (FNR)

False negative is referred as while a detection system fails to recognize a variance and categorized as benign. It is expressed as follows.

$$FNR = \frac{FN}{FN + TP}$$

Classification Rate (CR) or Accuracy

CR is computed by measuring how the detection system accurately detects IoT malwares and it is also described in terms of percentage of correctly detected IoT malwares from the entire dataset.

$$Accuracy = \frac{TP + TN}{TP + TN + FP + FN}$$

4.4 SUMMARY

Convolutional Neural Networks have shown great improvement in terms of detecting objects, learning patterns etc., are highly capable to learn and analyze complex real-world scenarios. Hence, this research utilized Deep Learning Algorithm (DLA) for forgery detection. From the Figure 4.11 and 4.12, as stated it is shown that the proposed algorithms outperform all the state of the art model with greater than 92% in overall accuracy. Experimental results as stated are the evidence for it. From this experimentation, it is observed that the previous available forensic tools used to analyze the video/image exploit content-based features. Furthermore, technically, the deep learning networks architecture designed to extract features meaningful for classification i.e. the ones which minimize the loss function are robust and improvised to the max using Optical flow. This practice is very common and in fact it is one of the fundamental steps in Deep Learning Algorithms (DLA).

Overtime, DLA's have improved and now are even capable of surpassing human abilities in detecting objects in images/videos when trained with an efficient dataset and an algorithm which keeps improving overtime tuning its hyper-parameters.

CHAPTER 5

CONCLUSION AND FUTURE WORK

This research proposed various schemes for ensuring IoT Security. Hence this dissertation proposes three novel schemes.

First scheme proposed is completely related to an IoT intrusion detection framework by adopting Artificial Intelligence and Edge computing technologies. It mainly concentrated on issues of data breaches and information insecurity because of slower data processing. It aims for effective threat detection by maintaining the integrity of security essentials in between IoT applications and its IoT ecosystem. Quality of Service (QoS) is improved by decreasing latency of IoT communication. Proposed framework's automated feature helps in the avoidance of manual intervention errors. It is light weighted and combat against data obfuscation techniques of intruders with the implementation of AI's privacy preserving techniques. Experimental results provide better results than earlier approaches, which implies effective and efficient IoT threat detection.

The second research work presented Deep Learning based security model IoT ecosytem by implementing Artificial Intelligence. As IoT ecosystem is incorporated with enormous amount of data, it is involved with several kinds of attacks by the malicious attackers by targeting the security loopholes of IoT ecosystem and devices. As per latest reports, more data breaching and privacy preserving attacks are happening in recent days especially during COVID - 19 periods. This work studied existing recent research works and observed the recent trending attacks of IoT ecosystem to build a novel DL based model. Further neural network auto encoders are utilized for effective prediction of attacks. UNSW-NB15 and Bot-IoT datasets are utilized for proposed model's validation and the performance of the model is evaluated using the standard performance metrics such as accuracy, precision, recall and F1 score. Experiment results show better results than previous works.

The third work fully focuses on AI based Fuzzy Logic Systems (AIFLS). IoT ecosystem is vast, it is emerged with enormous volume of data, devices, and equipment where all are interconnected through internet. This kind of interconnectivity increases the possibility of more types of attacks of malicious attackers who are eagerly aiming the security shortcomings related to IoT ecosystem as well as devices. Number of attack instances reached its apex level in the back to back pandemic periods of COVID - 19. In this work, secured malware detection framework is presented for IoT ecosystem on the basis of AIFLS. Automatic fuzzy logic rules generation is implemented. In addition, IoT malware classification is fastened and accurate by adopting Fuzzy Pattern Trees (FPT). UNSW-NB15 and Bot-IoT datasets are employed for validating proposed framework and its performance is assessed making use of the standard performance measures like TPR, FPR, FNR and Classification Rate. Experiment results depicts that improved results are attained by the proposed framework while comparing with existing recent research works. Figures displayed in the result analysis ensures that the performance analysis plot of the proposed framework.

Vital Problem addressed in this dissertation:

- Developed an autonomous malware detection and attack detection framework for IoT architecture.

- Developed an intelligent for IoT attack detection framework using effective Edge AI based computing.

- Developed an automated security model for data driven IoT ecosystem.

- Developed a secured IoT malware detection framework using AI based Fuzzy Logic Systems.

- Developed a novel AI based framework which is of first kind to deploy in real time.

- The problem of real time malware detection is developed and presented in this thesis.

Future Work

Future IoT system will able to detect the threats and attacks very quickly using the dynamic ways of prediction methods. This dynamic method is capable of capturing a new zero-day malwares and vulnerabilities on the IoT systems to mitigate these threats by applying the new techniques. The future IoT system should also be able to protect the data in the form of network across their boundaries. To protect the privacy from the user nodes, while fining the huge amount of data from the various nodes present in the network, new form of data analytics algorithms is developed and also to protect the hardware devices by developing the new cryptography methods. The risk management and assessment is another major problem in IoT devices because of the entire life-cycle of complex nodes present in the architecture. By addressing these issues in future, the risk management and assessment system needs a new technology to collect the data and processing a data in a secure manner using dynamic performance through online threat-based system may develop to avoid the attacks.

The Machine learning and deep learning algorithms are used to analyses the malwares on the real time scenario. The algorithms proposed in this dissertation are very much powerful for detecting the malware from the benign device. Therefore, the IoT device can easily protect from the attacker by comparing the already existing threats and vulnerabilities in an available dataset. The adversarial attacks can easily compromise the IoT device and bring down the learning data by controlling the behaviour of the learning methods. The new type of risk management is developed and security protocols are needed to detect the early warning in the future.

The test and monitor based system are needed for the IoT device, because the nodes from the various clusters are simultaneously sends the data from the various nodes. So, new audit policies that supports dynamic assessment in real-time security IoT system will be needed. This method is very useful for all the heterogeneous network components by using a wide range of solutions, minimal invasive and lightweight approach is essential in future IoT devices.

The next generation IoT security is based on the data confidentially using various methods like Homomorphic encryption and searchable encryption. The Homomorphic method is used to protect the data in the form of cipher text by encrypting the data. The searchable encryption method allows a storage data provider in the form of keywords or unpredictable patterns. This method will help to protect the data on a IoT device/network.

REFERENCES

1. Agiollo, A, Conti, M, Kaliyar, P, Lin, TN & Pajola, L 2021, 'DETONAR: Detection of Routing Attacks in RPL-Based IoT,' proceedings of IEEE Transactions on Network and Service Management, vol. 18, no. 2, pp. 1178-1190.

2. Ahmed, M & Pathan, ASK 2020, 'False data injection attack (FDIA): an overview and new metrics for fair evaluation of its countermeasure. Complex Adapt Syst Model, vol. 8, no.4.

3. Akram, H, Dimitri, K & Mohammed, M 2018, 'A comprehensive iot attacks survey based on a building-blocked reference mode', Int J AdvComputSciAppl.

4. Al-Garadi, MA, Mohamed, A, Al-Ali, AK, Du, X, Ali, I & Guizani, M 2020, 'A Survey of Machine and Deep Learning Methods for Internet of Things (IoT) Security,' proceedings of IEEE Communications Surveys & Tutorials, vol. 22, no. 3, pp. 1646-1685.

5. Al-Garadi, MA, Mohamed, A, Al-Ali, AK, Du, X, Ali, I, Guizani, M 2020, 'A Survey of Machine and Deep Learning Methods for Internet of Things (IoT) Security,' proceedings of IEEE Communications Surveys & Tutorials, vol. 22, no. 3, pp. 1646-1685.

6. Angrishi, K 2017, 'Turning internet of things (iot) into internet of vulnerabilities (iov): Iot botnets', CoRR, vol. abs/1702.03681.

7. Azmoodeh, A, Dehghantanha, A, Conti, M & Choo, KKR 2018, 'Detecting crypto-ransomware in IoT networks based on energy consumption footprint. J. Ambient Intell. Humaniz. Comput. vol. 9, no. 4, pp. 1141–1152.

8. Bhayo, J, Hameed, S & Shah, SA 2020, 'An Efficient Counter-Based DDoS Attack Detection Framework Leveraging Software Defined IoT (SD-IoT),' proceedings of IEEE Access, vol. 8, pp. 221612-221631.

9. Booij, TM, Chiscop, I, Meeuwissen, E, Moustafa, N & Hartog, FTHD 'ToN_IoT: The Role of Heterogeneity and the Need for Standardization of Features and Attack Types in IoT Network Intrusion

Data Sets,' proceedings of IEEE Internet of Things Journal, vol. 9, no. 1, pp. 485-496.

10. Bricker Bot Malware emerges, permanently bricks iot devices. Trend Micro, Trend Micro Incorporated. http://www.trend micro .com/vinfo /us/security/news/internet-of-thing s/brick erbot -malware-permanently-brick s-iot-devices. Accessed 19 Apr 2017.

11. Chaabouni, N, Mosbah, M, Zemmari, A, Sauvignac, C & Faruki, P 2019, 'Network Intrusion Detection for IoT Security Based on Learning Techniques,'proceedings of IEEE Communications Surveys & Tutorials, vol. 21,no. 3, pp. 2671-2701.

12. Das, AK, Bera, B, Wazid, M, Jamal, SS & Park, Y 2021, 'On the Security of a Secure and Lightweight Authentication Scheme for Next Generation IoT Infrastructure,' proceedings of IEEE Access, vol. 9, pp. 71856-71867.

13. Dib, M, Torabi, S, Bou-Harb, E & Assi, C 2021, 'A Multi-Dimensional Deep Learning Framework for IoT Malware Classification and Family Attribution,' proceedings of IEEE Transactions on Network and Service Management, vol. 18, no. 2, pp. 1165-1177.

14. Dinakarrao, SMP et al, 'Cognitive and Scalable Technique for Securing IoT Networks against Malware Epidemics,' proceedings of IEEE Access, vol. 8, pp. 138508-138528.

15. Doshi, K, Yilmaz, Y & Uludag, S 2021, 'Timely Detection and Mitigation of Stealthy DDoS Attacks Via IoT Networks,' proceedings of IEEE Transactions on Dependable and Secure Computing, vol. 18, no. 5, pp. 2164-2176.

16. Dushku, E, Rabbani, MM, Conti, M, Mancini, LV & Ranise, S 2020, 'SARA: Secure Asynchronous Remote Attestation for IoT Systems,' proceedings of IEEE Transactions on Information Forensics and Security, vol. 15, pp. 3123-3136.

17. Farahani, S 2008, 'Chapter 3 - zigbee and ieee 802.15.4 protocol layers', in ZigBeeWireless Networks and Transceivers, S. Farahani, Ed, Burlington: Newnes, pp. 33 –135, ISBN: 978-0-7506-8393-7.

18. Fernandes, E, Rahmati, A, Jung, J & Prakash, A 2017, 'Security implications of permission models in smart-home application frameworks', IEEE Security &Privacy, vol. 15, no. 2, pp. 24–30.

19. George, G & Thampi, SM 2018, 'A Graph-Based Security Framework for Securing Industrial IoT Networks From Vulnerability Exploitations,' in *IEEE Access*, vol. 6, pp. 43586-43601.

20. Ghahramani, M. Javidan, R. Shojafar, M. Taheri, R. Alazab, M. and Tafazolli, R 2021, 'RSS: An Energy-Efficient Approach for Securing IoT Service Protocols Against the DoS Attack,' proceedings of IEEE Internet of Things Journal, vol. 8, no. 5, pp. 3619-3635.

21. Granjal, J, Monteiro, E & Silva, JS 2015, 'Security for the Internet of Things: A survey of existing protocols and open research issues', IEEE Commun. Surveys Tuts, vol. 17, no. 3, pp. 1294-1312.

22. Haddadpajouh, H, Mohtadi, A, Dehghantanaha, A, Karimipour, H, Lin, X & Choo, KKR 2021, 'A Multikernel and Metaheuristic Feature Selection Approach for IoT Malware Threat Hunting in the Edge Layer,' proceedings of IEEE Internet of Things Journal, vol. 8, no. 6, pp. 4540-4547.

23. Hassan & Wan Haslina 2019, 'Current research on Internet of Things (IoT) security: A survey', Computer networks, vol. 148, pp. 283-294.

24. Hassija, V, Chamola, V, Saxena, V, Jain, D, Goyal, P & Sikdar, B 2019, 'A Survey on IoT Security: Application Areas, Security Threats, and Solution Architectures,' proceedings of IEEE Access, vol. 7, pp. 82721-82743.

25. Hossain, M & Xie, J 2020, 'Third Eye: Context-Aware Detection for Hidden Terminal Emulation Attacks in Cognitive Radio-Enabled IoT Networks,' proceedings of IEEE Transactions on Cognitive Communications and Networking, vol. 6, no. 1, pp. 214-228.

26. https://cybersecurity.att.com/blogs/labs-research/att-alien-labs-finds-new-golang-malwarebotenago-targeting-millions-of-routers-and-iot-devices-with-more-than-30 exploits?utm.

27. Hussain, F et al, 2021, 'A Two-Fold Machine Learning Approach to Prevent and Detect IoT Botnet Attacks,' proceedigs of IEEE Access, vol. 9, pp. 163412-163430.

28. Hussain, F, Hussain, R, Hassan, SA & Hossain, E 2020, 'Machine Learning in IoT Security: Current Solutions and Future Challenges,' in IEEE Communications Surveys & Tutorials, vol. 22, no. 3, pp. 1686-1721.

29. Iqbal, H, Abbas, W, Daneshmand, M, Rauf, B & Bangash, YA 2020, 'An In-Depth Analysis of IoT Security Requirements, Challenges, and Their Counter measures via Software-Defined Security,' in IEEE Internet of Things Journal, vol. 7, no. 10, pp. 10250-10276, Oct.

30. Iqbal, W, Abbas, H, Daneshmand, M, Rauf, B & Bangash, YA 2020, 'An In-Depth Analysis of IoT Security Requirements, Challenges, and Their Countermeasures via Software-Defined Security,' proceedings of IEEE Internet of Things Journal, vol. 7, no. 10, pp. 10250-10276, Oct.

31. Jeon, J, Park, JH & Jeong, YS 2020, 'Dynamic Analysis for IoT Malware Detection with Convolution Neural Network Model,' proceedings of IEEE Access, vol. 8, pp. 96899-96911.

32. Jeon, J, Park, JH & Jeong, YS 2020, 'Dynamic Analysis for IoT Malware Detection with Convolution Neural Network Model,' proceedings of IEEE Access, vol. 8, pp. 96899-96911.

33. Jia, Y, Zhong, F, Alrawais, A, Gong, B & Cheng, X 2020, 'FlowGuard: An Intelligent Edge Defense Mechanism Against IoT DDoS Attacks,' proceedings of IEEE Internet of Things Journal, vol. 7, no. 10, pp. 9552-9562.

34. Jurn J, Kim T, Kim H. An automated vulnerability detection and remediation method for software security. Sustainability. 10:1652.

35. Kayastha, N, Niyato, D, Hossain, E & Han, Z 2014, 'Smart grid sensor data collection, communication, and networking: A tutorial', Wireless Communications and Mobile Computing, vol. 14, no.11, pp. 1055–1087.

36. Khan, AY, Latif, R, Latif, S, Tahir, S, Batool, G & Saba, T 2020, 'Malicious Insider Attack Detection in IoTs Using Data Analytics,' proceedings of IEEE Access, vol. 8, pp. 11743-11753.

37. Khanam, S, Ahmedy, IB, Idna Idris, MY Jaward, MH & Bin MdSabri, AQ 2020, 'A Survey of Security Challenges, Attacks Taxonomy and

Advanced Countermeasures in the Internet of Things,' proceedings of IEEE Access, vol. 8, pp. 219709-219743.

38. Langner, R 2011, 'Stuxnet: dissecting a cyberwarfare weapon,' IEEE Security & Privacy Magazine, vol. 9, no. 3, pp. 49–51.

39. Lei, X, Tu, G, Liu, AX, Li, C & Xie, T 2018, 'The insecurity of home digital voice assistants - vulnerabilities, attacks and countermeasures', proceedings of 2018 IEEE Conference on Communications and Network Security (CNS), pp. 1–9.

40. Lins, FAA & Vieira, M 2021, 'Security Requirements and Solutions for IoT Gateways: A Comprehensive Study,' proceedings of IEEE Internet of Things Journal, vol. 8, no. 11, pp. 8667-8679.

41. Liu, Y, Ma, M, Liu, X, Xiong, NN, Liu, A & Zhu, Y 2020, 'Design and Analysis of Probing Route to Defense Sink-Hole Attacks for Internet of Things Security,' proceedings of IEEE Transactions on Network Science and Engineering, vol. 7, no. 1, pp. 356-372.

42. Lounis, K & Zulkernine, 2020, 'Attacks and Defenses in Short-Range Wireless Technologies for IoT,' proceedings of IEEE Access, vol. 8, pp. 88892-88932.

43. Makhdoom, I, Abolhasan, M, Lipman, J, Liu, RP & Ni, W 2019, 'Anatomy of Threats to the Internet of Things,' proceedings of IEEE Communications Surveys & Tutorials, vol. 21, no. 2, pp. 1636-1675.

44. Mazhar, N, Salleh, R, Zeeshan, M & Hameed, MM 2021, 'Role of Device Identification and Manufacturer Usage Description in IoT Security: A Survey,' proceedings of IEEE Access, vol. 9, pp. 41757-41786.

45. Meidan, Y, Bohadana, M, Shabtai, A, Ochoa, M, Tippenhauer, NO, Guarnizo, JD & Elovici, Y 2017, 'Detection of unauthorized IoT devices using machine learning techniques'.

46. Melamed, T 2018, 'An active man-in-the-middle attack on bluetooth smart devices', WIT Press, International Journal of Safety and Security Engineering. http://www.witpr ess.com/elibrary/sse-volum es/8/2/2120. Accessed 1 Feb.

47. Meneghello, F, Calore, M, Zucchetto, D, Polese, M & Zanella, A 2019, 'IoT: Internet of Threats? A Survey of Practical Security Vulnerabilities in Real IoT Devices,' proceedings of IEEE Internet of Things Journal, vol. 6, no. 5, pp. 8182-8201.

48. Mishra, N & Pandya, S 2021, 'Internet of Things Applications, Security Challenges, Attacks, Intrusion Detection, and Future Visions: A Systematic Review,' proceedings of IEEE Access, vol. 9, pp. 59353-59377.

49. Mohammed, H, Hasan, SR & Awwad, F 2020, 'Fusion-On-Field Security and Privacy Preservation for IoT Edge Devices: Concurrent Defense against Multiple Types of Hardware Trojan Attacks,' proceedings of IEEE Access, vol. 8, pp. 36847-36862.

50. Morgner, P, Mattejat, S & Benenson, Z 2016, 'All your bulbs are belong to us: Investigating the current state of security in connected lighting systems', CoRR, vol. abs/1608.03732.

51. Nasralla, MM, García-Magariño, I & Lloret, J 2020, 'Defenses Against Perception-Layer Attacks on IoT Smart Furniture for Impaired People,' proceedings of IEEE Access, vol. 8, pp. 119795-119805.

52. Neshenko, N, Bou-Harb, E, Crichigno, J, Kaddoum, G, Ghani, N 2019, 'Demystifying IoT Security: An Exhaustive Survey on IoT Vulnerabilities and a First Empirical Look on Internet-Scale IoT Exploitations,' proceedings of IEEE Communications Surveys & Tutorials, vol. 21, no. 3, pp. 2702-2733.

53. Petrov, C 2019, Internet Of things statistics from 2019 to justify the rise of IoT (2019).

54. Rana, MM & Bo, R 2019, 'IoT-Based Improved Human Motion Estimations Method Under Cyber Attacks,' proceedings of IEEE Internet of Things Journal, vol. 6, no. 6, pp. 10934-10935.

55. Raoof, A, Matrawy, A & Lung, CH 2019, 'Routing Attacks and Mitigation Methods for RPL-Based Internet of Things,' proceedings of IEEE Communications Surveys & Tutorials, vol. 21, no. 2, pp. 1582-1606.

56. Ravi, N & Shalinie, SM 2020, 'Semisupervised-Learning-Based Security to Detect and Mitigate Intrusions in IoT Network,'

proceedings of IEEE Internet of Things Journal, vol. 7, no. 11, pp. 11041-11052.

57. Rodrigues, B 2015, 'Arris cable modem has a backdoor in the backdoor, https://w00tsec.blogspot.com/2015/11/arris-cable-modem-has-backdoor-in.html.

58. Sakhnini, J, Karimipour, H, Dehghantanha, A, Parizi, RM & Srivastava, G 2019, Security aspects of internet of things aided smart grids: a bibliometric survey. Internet Things, vol. 100111.

59. Sathyadevan, S, Achuthan, K, Doss, R & Pan, L 2019, 'Protean Authentication Scheme – A Time-Bound Dynamic KeyGen Authentication Technique for IoT Edge Nodes in Outdoor Deployments,' proceedings of IEEE Access, vol. 7, pp. 92419-92435.

60. Sfar, Arbia Riahi, Enrico Natalizio, Yacine Challal & Zied Chtourou 2018, 'A roadmap for security challenges in the Internet of Things,' Digital Communications and Networks, vol. 4, no. 2, pp. 118-137.

61. Shafiq, M, Tian, Z, Bashir, AK, Du, X & Guizani, M 2021, 'CorrAUC: A Malicious Bot-IoT Traffic Detection Method in IoT Network Using Machine-Learning Techniques,' proceedings of IEEE Internet of Things Journal, vol. 8, no. 5, pp. 3242-3254.

62. Sharma, V, You, I, Andersson, K, Palmieri, F, Rehmani, MH & Lim, J 2020, 'Security, Privacy and Trust for Smart Mobile- Internet of Things (M-IoT): A Survey,' proceedings of IEEE Access, vol. 8, pp. 167123-167163.

63. Simplício, MA, Silva, MVM Alves, RCA & Shibata, TKC 'Lightweight and escrow-less authenticated key agreement for the internet of things', Comput. Commun, vol. 98, pp. 43–51.

64. Sood, K, Karmakar, KK, Yu, S, Varadharajan, V, Pokhrel, SR & Xiang, Y 2020, 'Alleviating Heterogeneity in SDN-IoT Networks to Maintain QoS and Enhance Security,' proceedings of IEEE Internet of Things Journal, vol. 7, no. 7, pp. 5964-5975.

65. Spreitzer, R, Moonsamy, V, Korak, T & Mangard, S 2018, 'Systematic classification of side-channel attacks: A case study for mobile devices', IEEE Communications Surveys Tutorials, vol. 20, no. 1, pp. 465–488.

66. Stoffer, V 2013, 'Outdated computers and operating systems'.

67. Stone, J 2019, 'A flaw in amazon's ring doorbells leaked customers' wi-fi credentials', Cyberscoop.

68. Sudhakaran & Pradeep 2021, 'Detection of Malware from IOT Devices Using Deep Learning Techniques,' Journal of Physics: Conference Series, vol. 1818, no. 1, IOP Publishing.

69. Sudheera, KLK, Divakaran, DM, Singh, RP & Gurusamy, M 2021,'ADEPT: Detection and Identification of Correlated Attack Stages in IoT Networks,' proceedings of IEEE Internet of Things Journal, vol. 8, no. 8, pp. 6591-6607, 15 April.

70. Torabi, S, Dib, M, Bou-Harb, E, Assi, C & Debbabi, M 2021, 'A Strings-Based Similarity Analysis Approach for Characterizing IoT Malware and Inferring Their Underlying Relationships,' proceedings of IEEE Networking Letters, vol. 3, no. 3, pp. 161-165.

71. Ullah & Mahmoud, QH 2021, 'Design and Development of a Deep Learning-Based Model for Anomaly Detection in IoT Networks,' in IEEE Access, vol. 9, pp. 103906-103926.

72. Vasan, D, Alazab, M, Venkatraman, S, Akram, J & Qin, Z 2020, 'MTHAEL: Cross-Architecture IoT Malware Detection Based on Neural Network Advanced Ensemble Learning,' proceedings of IEEE Transactions on Computers, vol. 69, no. 11, pp. 1654-1667.

73. Wang, J 2021, et al, 'IoT-Praetor: Undesired Behaviours Detection for IoT Devices,' proceedings of IEEE Internet of Things Journal, vol. 8, no. 2, pp. 927-940.

74. Wazid, M, Das, AK, Rodrigues, JJPC, Shetty, S & Park, Y 'IoMT Malware Detection Approaches: Analysis and Research Challenges,' proceedings of IEEE Access, vol. 7, pp. 182459-182476.

75. Xenofontos, C, Zografopoulos, I, Konstantinou, C, Jolfaei, A, Khan, MK & Choo, KKR 2022, 'Consumer, Commercial, and Industrial IoT (In)Security: Attack Taxonomy and Case Studies,' proceedings of IEEE Internet of Things Journal, vol. 9, no. 1, pp. 199-221.

76. Xiang, X. Cao, J & Fan, W 2021, 'Scalable Attestation Protocol Resilient to Physical Attacks for IoT Environments,' proceedings of IEEE Systems Journal, vol. 15, no. 3, pp. 4566-4577.

77. Yang, N, Chen, K & Wang, M 2021, 'SmartDetour: Defending Blackhole and Content Poisoning Attacks in IoT NDN Networks,' proceedings of IEEE Internet of Things Journal, vol. 8, no. 15, pp. 12119-12136.

78. Yi, M, Xu, X & Xu, L 2019, 'An Intelligent Communication Warning Vulnerability Detection Algorithm Based on IoT Technology,' in IEEE Access, vol. 7, pp. 164803-164814.

79. Zhang, N, Wu, R, Yuan, S, Yuan, C & Chen, D 2019, 'RAV: Relay Aided Vectorized Secure Transmission in Physical Layer Security for Internet of Things Under Active Attacks,' proceeidngs of IEEE Internet of Things Journal, vol. 6, no. 5, pp. 8496-8506, Oct.

80. Zhang, W, Zhang, B, Zhou, Y, He, H & Ding, Z 2020, 'An IoT Honeynet Based on Multiport Honeypots for Capturing IoT Attacks,' in IEEE Internet of Things Journal, vol. 7, no. 5, pp. 3991-3999, May.

81. Zhou, Y, Cheng, G & Yu, S 2021, 'An SDN-Enabled Proactive Defense Framework for DDoS Mitigation in IoT Networks,' proceedings of IEEE Transactions on Information Forensics and Security, vol. 16, pp. 5366-5380.

82. https://www.cloudflare.com/en-in/learning/ddos/glossary/mirai-botnet/.

83. https://www.f5.com/labs/articles/cisotociso/ai-powered-cyber-attacks.

84. https://www.globalsign.com/en/blog/man-in-the-middle-attacks-iot.

85. https://www.marketsandmarkets.com/pdfdownloadNew.asp?id=573.

86. https://www.sonicwall.com/news/new-sonicwall-research-finds-aggressive-growth-in-ransomware-rise-in-iot-attacks/.

87. https://www.trgdatacenters.com/what-is-a-permanent-dos-pdos-attack-and-can-i-stop-it/.

88. cdn.iotwf.com/resources/72/IoT_Reference_Model_04_June_2014.pdf

Milton Keynes UK
Ingram Content Group UK Ltd.
UKHW050258020324
438623UK00011B/518

9 781835 80094